TALKIES

Poetry
New Chatto Poets II (a contributor)
A Scottish Assembly
Sharawaggi (with W. N. Herbert)
Other Tongues: Young Scottish Poets in English, Scots and
Gaelic (editor)

Literary Criticism
The Savage and the City in the Work of T. S. Eliot
Devolving English Literature
About Edwin Morgan (co-editor with Hamish Whyte)
The Arts of Alasdair Gray (co-editor with Thom Nairn)
Reading Douglas Dunn (co-editor with David Kinloch)

TALKIES

Robert Crawford

Chatto & Windus
LONDON

Published in 1992 by
Chatto & Windus Ltd
20 Vauxhall Bridge Road
London SW1V 2SA

Second Impression 1994

A CIP catalogue record for this book is available from the
British Library.

ISBN 0 7011 3928 5

Photoset by
Cambridge Composing (UK) Ltd
Cambridge

Printed in Great Britain
by Mackays of Chatham PLC,
Chatham, Kent

Acknowledgements

Some of these poems have appeared in *Alumnus Chronicle,
Gairfish, Interference, Krino, London Magazine, London
Review of Books, The New Makars, New Writing Scotland,
Oxford Poetry, Poetry Book Society Anthology, Poetry
Review, Quadrant, Somhairle, Soho Square IV and Squibs*.
Others have been broadcast on BBC Radio 4's *Poetry Now*.
The author is grateful to all the editors involved.

The publisher acknowledges subsidy from the Scottish
Arts Council towards the publication of this volume.

For Alice
with love

Contents

'. . . one's own language is never a single language . . .'

M. M. Bakhtin

CHEVALIER

The voice is holed up in a cave. Water drips on it. Silent,
Despised men keep watch outside.

The voice in the heather, disguised as a woman, moves
Mostly at night. Money's available

For information about the voice. Vessels
Wait all day offshore, listening.

The voice is nearly inaudible on a tiny island. Sun beats
   down on its vowels.
People are burned out for the voice, which sheds

Enough clothes for many generations. They festoon
   museums.
It gets so quiet searchers hear nothing,

Can't even tell its language. The voice escapes
To Argentina and Cape Breton Island, gets drunk,

Mouthing obscenities, toasting itself
Over and over. Silence doesn't chasten it.

Rewards and spies increase. The voice
Loses consciousness, won't be betrayed.

D'ARCY

He wore an old jacket because his passenger
Liked to claw and bill into the tweed.

As he passed along South Street towards the Owl House
Children brought dead birds, shocking him

By not knowing their names – chaffinch, *fringilla coelebs*;
Cinclus cinclus, dipper or water ousel. Once a storm

Blew the pinioned lime-green wings across three gardens.
'Professor Thompson wants his parrot back.'

He wore it home. It spoke. It sang his name,
'D'Arcy, D'Arcy,' as he wrote his thesis

On form in evolution, cackling and sipping
Sometimes a dram, or a glass of Hirondelle.

TALKIES

Already there is gossip in Hollywood
About something new. Even the stars will need tests.

In the beginning was the caption,
Ringlets, a balletic flow of knees;

Crowds opened their mouths, then closed them.
Now some will never be heard of again

If between camera-loving, soundless lips
Is a foreign accent, or that timbre of voice which means

The microphone doesn't like you.
Friends swell into enormous heart-throbs:

Their voices are good. 'Retraining?
Let me get you another drink.'

At the neat wrought-iron table,
Legs crossed, she stares at the studio,

A hangar, a camp, a silo. Work
Means something else now, something other

Than what she set her heart on, black and white silk,
    panache.
With a longer lifespan she might become

A nostalgia executive, a Last of the, a rediscovery.
But the dates are wrong; leaving her speechless

At this technology crackling over California
Eagerly, far out of sight.

SIMULTANEOUS TRANSLATION

It fills up the pause when you finish speaking,
Or even before you've stopped,

Gets between the chewy biro and the word-processor,
Between 'Yours sincerely' and your name.

Other times you walk right into it
At Aberfeldy, going over the Highland Line

Towards something you can't understand,
Also somewhere you've been.

Gaels in Glasgow, Bangladeshis in Bradford,
Negotiators, opera-buffs, tourists:

This is where we all live now,
Wearing something like a Sony Walkman,

Hearing another voice every time we speak.
A girl opens her mouth and an Oxbridge bass

Is talking in English. What is she really saying?
Already her finger is starting to creep

Closer to the binding of a parallel text,
Between the lines, then crossing over.

KYPIE

Ut's guid manners i Strathgowkie
Tae speak o 'manky Strathgawkie'
In Strathgawkie yi huv tae say
'yon sae-caa'd Strathgowkie'

When Strathgawkers or Strathgowkers
blether aboot jinin thegither
an a tourist hinks baith
waant thi wan hing

then Strathgowkers mean
victory o Strathgowkery
an Strathgawkers waant
Total Strathgawkinization

Best no tae mess
Wi Strathgawkers or Strathgowkers
Baith aye tak tent
o ivry wurd yi say

Ambassates o third fourth
an fift an furder countries
mind weel tae learn thi rules an yawn
tae hear o Strathgawkie-Strathgowkie

eftir thi German o thi Austrian Erich Fried

kypie – a man who uses his left hand instead of his right

ACCIDENTS

Evening slinks in over Cummertrees.
After centuries of feuding, the names of Scotland and
    England

Have settled down, so this side of the quicksands Carlyle
Means *Sartor Resartus*; on the other side, Carlisle.

Patriots get huffy, seeing the hills over there
Look just like our own and shrug off what we call them:

Sellafield, Windscale. Just after lunch
I'm reading how the name of Henry Duncan

Links the savings bank movement to the first scientific
    treatise
On fossilized footprints. Clatteringshaws Loch, Haugh of
    Urr

Trip lazily past, and images of cooling towers'
Bloated hourglasses slough away as we drive

To sleep together at Beeswing, chosen from the
    guidebook almost
But not quite at random, just because we treasure the
    name.

STASH

To know is to slip your hand inside
A secret place, and close on the roundness of glass,

The neck of a bottle in its darkened niche,
An unsmashed Reformation saint.

To know is to detect
Telltale signs: stains, wheeltracks,

Smeek of rich, spirituous fires,
Vestiges of creation.

*

Outsiders come to trap that knowledge,
Bearing down on the spirit's vessels

With the weight of the law, but the makers are too light-
    footed.
They gather up their gleaming test-tubes,

Camouflage fires, cram their bottles
Down rock-fissures too remote and obstinate

For the hands of the Revenue to reach between roots.
A slow, patient, moony Resistance

Lies in wait for the throats of children,
Ready to rage and confer its blessing

That till now is illicit and still.

BARRA

At night you are a collie stretched on the waters.
Kisimul Castle is your dish.

The plane that growls across the cocklestrand
Would hold the Presbyterians of this Catholic island

Each of whom was eagerly praying on Sunday
For the conversion of India and China.

In the Craigard men talk fish through the news,
There is silence for the weather forecast.

Drams vanish down a boilersuited Rembrandt
Who works on the Vatersay road,

First asphalt on this continent that begins with Gaelic,
Playing snooker, trussing sheep in the back of a van.

Out there in that dog's dish of a castle
Is where the herald proclaimed from the battlements,

'Macneil of Barra has had his dinner.
The rest of the world may now dine.'

MARY OF BERNERA

Mary of Bernera, doe-eyed Mary, Mary of the songs, you are as honey and your breasts are as sweet white apples, but I no longer find you erotically attractive. When the Minister of the Free Church preached his sermon against my hands inside your bathing dress I was in the kirk and was traumatized by it. All the energies which our love consumed I now devote to marketing edible seaweeds. Mary of Bernera, doe-eyed Mary, Mary of the songs, though I cannot be with you I have your eyelashes in a small box. I carry it with me to the sea's edge and on the shingle. I who was your lover now sell seaweed to old crofters from a Renault van. There is a matchbox in my overalls. Think on me, Mary of the songs.

BAPTISM

Only this morning he had not been arrested;
It was Lowlanders did it as a practical joke

He still can't quite understand.
He just wanted work, and now here he is

Bundled into the back seat of a Baby Austin
By two big Glasgow constables.

'Right, then, Donald, aff tae the station.'
Neither of the constables has the Gaelic.

LOST

They are sitting out on Europe's fingernails,
On the losing edge of a war.

In the new school and windswept houses
Radios are tuned to Mr Churchill

Speaking in English about France.
Unconsciously, some of the older ones

Translate 'their finest hour' into Gaelic.
Daydreaming of Hitler, and unharvested corn,

Girls pull headscarves tight round their cheekbones;
Everyone is waving, like on the Movietone News.

School-leavers recite Shakespeare's St Crispin's Day
    speech
But Somhairle MacGill-Eain will describe a dead boy

Near El Alamein in another tongue. Without men
There are only children keen for rare stamps,

Then yellow irises, gannets.

Z

The Greeks call him Zeta. Brigadier 'Fairy' Fairholme
Complains in his sleep about Zed,
But the US war correspondent in Athens
Ends every dispatch with wishful thinking:
'Chief agent Zee has been recalled.'

Z whispers a few words of Gaelic
To save time encoding. He can do imperrrsonations
Of Grrreat Lowland Scots. An Old Boy of St Paul's,
He likes to talk like his ex-headmaster
Addressing the lads, or convincing his governors

To up his salary by a thou.
Z was at Gallipoli. Henry James wrote him a letter
Urging him to take care. Z orders a single malt
At a Piraeus cafe, and thinks of how C
Sawed off his own leg with a pocket knife.

At first Z obeyed orders
To burn all his blotting paper, lest Baron Schenk von
    Schweinburg
Should decypher his notes with a mirror.
Now his tactics are a little different:
He has his own headed parchment, printed with an
    enormous Z,

And travels everywhere *molto cognito*
In an open-top Sunbeam, 'an Apollonian vehicle'.
Z likes his agents to wear the kilt
In sight of the Acropolis. Some wear the small Greek kilt,
Others ex-stock from the Seaforth Highlanders.

Z frequents the raciest nightclubs
Whose revues include monocled skits on himself
Reclining on plaid. The refrain of the chorus
Is 'Hush . . . here comes the bogeyman'.
Z guffaws in the very front row.

The Guardian says the future of English fiction
Is in the hands of Z. Under his tutelage
An ex-lavatory salesman obtains the letters
Of the King of Greece; an American short-story writer
Is appointed governor of one of the Cyclades, wearing a
    Seaforth kilt.

A piece of Cyclopean masonry
Crashes on to the hairpins just behind the full-throttle
    Sunbeam.
A wheel flies off. Z writes to his wife on Capri:
'Send me, please, two white suits (by Forster's),
My light-coloured ties, and the best of my new white felt
    hats.'

British diplomats call him the Pirate.
He started work as a clerk. Now his 'visa files'
Cover an eighth of the population of Athens
In *BOP* detail. At night he writes questions
For distribution to agents at dawn:

Who is Madame P? Does 'Tennyson'
Negotiate with 'Byron'? Is L's moustache his own?
Z organizes an ambush, the fake taxis crash,
The interceptor forgets his codename, the Kaiser's agent
    is 7 feet tall.
Z has to cosh him on the bonce himself,

But captures the message. He dashes upstairs
At the British School of Archaeology
To novelize his report,
And shouts from his window, 'Ahoy there, [*name
  withheld*],
Didn't we act together at Magdalen in *The Clouds*?'

Z quotes a line of Aristophanes
In several languages, drifting from one to the other
And feeling each change him, sensing how they all make
  him up
Sitting on a cane chair at an upstairs window,
Sunlight ribbing the shutters.

Z speculates on the Pictish Z-rod,
Symbol of no one's sure what. He smokes
Tobacco purloined from the King of Greece
And sets out for the HQ of M11(C)
Just above the Authors' Club in London

Where he tells C about the blown Black Hat spying
Over Islay malt. 'Good Lord, Z,
Your stuff should be published, if it wasn't so damned
  secret.
We're doubling your budget. Asquith thinks you're the
  tops.'
Z smiles and nods. He sees the beach at Gallipoli

And the corpses of pipers. Back in Athens he starts
Another novel – *No Papers* – but Hoffmann captures it,
Convinced it's in code. *Neo Hemera*
Prints front-page stories about Z's longings
For a new Greek Empire, 'the Greece of Goodwin's
  Grammar'.

He commandeers Prince George's royal yacht
For a tour of the islands, keeping on deck
Two large sacks each of which contains
A very close friend of Enver Pasha
And a hefty rock. He accepts the Legion d'Honneur

As his enemies close in. Ex-Oxford dons,
One an old Proctor who remembers Z
Dropping a shoe on a policeman,
Sweep grandly on board, and are bought off for a time
By being given a shot at the steering,

But they cable home: 'Z's outfit nothing more
Than a theatrical tour. His intelligence rubbish.
Might make a second-in-command.'
Z plops ice-cubes into his whisky. He plays with his
    swordstick.
He knows that things are not well,

And starts to imagine another life
Among different islands: the Outer Hebrides, maybe,
Where in future he will set up a great
Green gramophone horn on the isle of Barra,
Broadcasting Bruckner to the Minch.

He had not yet become a Scottish nationalist,
Or been knighted, or travelled India,
But when Professor Lawson snaps, 'You're finished, Z –
End of your alphabet,' the man retorts
'Neither in Greek, nor in Pictish',

Then about-turns from the yacht's saloon,
Out along her foredeck, then (some of this is untrue)
Over the rail and across the Aegean
North through Europe to the cocklestrand and Eoligarry
Where the piper drops dead at his funeral.

RADIO SCOTTISH DEMOCRACY

You hear an old man scratching himself
Before he gets up at Kinlochmoidart.

You tune into a woman in Lima, yawning.
You listen to what hasn't happened yet, the shout

That is still just an intake of breath;
Straining so hard, your imagination

Becomes a microphone for the future.
A new voice starts to come unjammed

Against a rout of white-noise, Floddens,
Cullodens, nostalgias that rhyme,

When kilties went roaring over the grass,
Fell on it, let it grow through them.

You pick up words moving – towards or away?
Reaction times quicken. Is that it? Listen –

Not to dour centuries of trudging,
Marching, and taking orders;

Today I have heard the feet of my country
Breaking into a run.

WS

i.m. John L. Paterson

You listen at doors that are just ajar,
Can't make it out.

When you push, a kind of gauze
Stops them opening any further,

But you can hear by candlelight
The speech-rhythm of a people,

An inner Abbotsford of guesses:
What your father said at the '31 Derby,

How your wife laughed before you met her;
All those sparrows and hairs of the head,

Famous non-celebrities, characters not in Smollett,
Sources never to be revealed

Without whom you could neither speak nor listen,
To be taken on trust, the unquoted.

You are a writer, but not to the Signet.
Your job is to be at their hearings.

NAVAJO

Their breath petrifies, is sold as bookends.
Masonry topples into cowdung or hogans.
In native pickups across mile-high grazing
Radios try not to drop stitches
From a patchwork of local languages.

Bracelets made of the sky's turquoise
Replant burnt orchards; past purple flowers
Tourists head for medieval America
Silhouetted against the horizon,
Streamlined, woken abruptly.

THE DECLARATION OF ARBROATH

Arisaig is sly with the smell of catmint,
Discussion groups overflow Milngavie.

Buchanan, Mackenzie, MacNamarra,
Surnames on war-memorials remind me

Of bare names in a village near St Jean de Luce,
The young Basques who died for France.

For so long as there shall be but one hundred
Of us remain alive, we will never . . .

In Robert Burns's house at Dumfries
I saw the words 'The poet died in this bed'

Translated into thirty languages.
He'd take a can of petrol to his verses and letters,

Torch them, and scatter the acrid ashes
In a shopping mall, for self-respect.

GRAID

Graid (verb active) to make ready
Graid (past participle) made ready

(Jamieson's Dictionary of the Scottish Language)

The sea infiltrates the bays. Young women
Are telephone-selling in Gaelic and sound

All the more insistent because you don't know what
  you're buying.

Our stonechat population has not decreased;
These statistics are necessary.

A big crane balances a portion of Glasgow,
Puts it down, opts for a stronger one.

In this gloaming languages capsize
Into one another, creole as the buildings of Dumfries.

Your clock-radio sings you awake
With a different song every morning,

Saddling up today like a bleary Clydesdale,
Revving it like a Suzuki.

Under-bonnet laughter: the Peugeot manual quotes
  Confucius.
An accountant moves on when her software is all in
  place.

We were on the boat to Barra during the Russian coup:
Gorbachev, Caledonian MacBrayne,

And the flashing black and white of peewits
Rising from a crop of barley.

Only this January your mother died.
The new draft timetable is in the second drawer.

Preparations are afoot.

While living in the cave, the king spent several hours watching a spider. Trying to attach its web to the far side of the cave, the small creature repeatedly swung across but failed to make the contact it sought. It did not give up, but persisted until, eventually, it secured its goal. The king regarded this as a fit emblem for his own struggle. So it is that the spider came to be our national emblem, symbol of our resourcefulness and determination. That is why so many Scots (including a remarkable number of poets) have been called by the forename Spider.

The story of Sir David Brewster's invention of the kaleidoscope is too well-known to bear retelling here. What is less well-known is that because he was for some years Principal of St Andrews University, that is why our national kaleidoscope is known as the St Andrews Kaleidoscope. The massive kaleidoscope constructed at the centre of St Andrews is both fit memorial to Brewster and an appropriate emblem of the ever-changing energy of the Scottish people. Like the St Andrew's Cross or Saltire, the St Andrews Kaleidoscope is immediately recognized around the globe as a distinctive emblem of Scotland.

Because of the strictly Calvinistic character of the Scottish people, their national dress is peculiarly stark. The grey pinstripe trousers and black long-tailed jacket, the 'morningsuit' of the Presbyterian Elder, have been adopted since the eighteenth-century as our national costume, as befits a country where brightly-coloured or unusual clothing is generally viewed as sinful. Many famous Scottish regiments have been regarded with fear and awe by their enemies not least because of their distinctive garb. In World War One, a particular regiment achieved notoriety with the Kaiser's troops who nicknamed it 'the Elders from Hell'.

OTHER

Without you the seesaw wouldn't work,
There would be no borders. Teachers say it's wrong

To conceive you as cannibal, shrinking heads,
Kilted, with crinkly hair.

Travelling companion, I like to see
My bungalow, my country, my pale nose

Utterly strange, to speculate
On accidents of birth; you indulge me, other half,

Aboriginal, holding a kind of root
I grew from, staring back

With knife-sharpener's eyes never content
At being only imagined.

CUSTOMS

'*The Golden Bough* has been abridged
For the convenience of smugglers. It now fits a lady's
    handbag.
In any future plots against Sir James,
His works can be carried across national frontiers
To be buried in secret hiding places
He himself has chosen: the shores of the Lake of Nemi;
The sacred grove, Uppsala; the Braes of Balquhidder;
The Babar Archipelago.' So Lady Frazer
To The Brotherhood of the Golden Bough.

Sir James smiles. Blind as a seer
From Homeric times, he has encoded
His secret hates among the Fellows of Trinity
In the minutiae of the abridged edition
Alongside the names of girls from Helensburgh
He once wanted to sleep with: Helen Mackellar,
Fiona Simpson, Henrietta Walker.
He writes the words 'a dreamy voluptuous cult'.
Nobody has discovered them yet.

Lady Frazer learns masonic handshakes.
Her daughter dreams that she is Alan Breck
Lying silent, parched on top of a high rock,
With the redcoat soldiers below.
'Memories of the sister who sleeps in the land
Of Adonis never again to waken',
Sir James pauses and dips his pen
Into a mephitic pool of Quink,
'With the anemones and the roses.'

At night Lady Frazer flits like an owl
Among the rooftops of Cambridge, carrying her ear-
    trumpet,
Too-wooing to the sleepers, 'All of England shall pass'.

Sir James listens to the rustling skirts
Of his newest secretary, 'religious emotions
Of this sensuous, visionary sort', silky
Warm air currents waft from her legs, sending him
Like those young men at Kitty Hawk, North Carolina,
Gradually into the clouds.

He remembers his parents, his father compiling
A history of pens and paper. He remembers leading
The bull Mnevis of Heliopolis
Along East Argyle Street, tethering him to the porch.
He remembers climbing among the clump of trees
Where he perfected the ritual slaughter
Of Free Church elders, their dark, oozing blood
Staining and enriching all of Dunbartonshire,
Spirits of the Corn and the Wild.

There are similar practices in Orkney and Bavaria.
Adonis is an analogue of Rupert Brooke. Standing to
    address
Anthropologists in London, his eyes red over with blood,
He clutches his enormous napkin and falls.
Lady Frazer's electric hearing apparatus
Picks up signals from the Third Programme,
Broadcasting the vicious Stravinski. She grabs a steak-
    knife
And plunges it deep into the President
Of the Royal Society. 'Mussolini! Stalin!'

She yells, 'Come into this grove! Kill them
In the name of Sir James!' Officials
Rush towards the dinner table, dragging her screaming
    away.
Secretaries are dialling 999,
Demanding news-blackouts. Presbyterian hymns
Waft on the shore-wind, mixed with the peal of bells.
She writes pamphlets requiring the re-institution

Of seasonal killings and sacred prostitution.
She writes a history of the British Empire's

Cultivation of bloodsports. She is declared insane, locked
    up,
Lives several lifetimes, embraces the thought of Michel
    Foucault
Synthesized with the doctrine of reincarnation,
Claiming to be in constant astral contact
With Sir James himself, who is still dictating
Extra volumes of *The Golden Bough* which deal
With frontiers and warfare, the Oxbridge system,
Sir Walter Scott's sacrifice of Border virgins,
Television's ritual banality.

The rights of these books are all bought up
By titled people, media tycoons.
Not a word is ever published.
She reads and re-reads her husband's works:
'Ta-uz, who is no other than Tammuz, is here
Like Burns's John Barleycorn.' She cries
Over *Tristes Tropiques*. She writes the story
Of herself as she would have been if Compton Mackenzie
Had not invented visas as a method of surveillance,

If the Judeao-Christian tradition and Newtonian physics
Had not attempted to normalize and censor
Human behaviour, if poststructuralism
Had formed the basis of all human cuisine, and if Byron
Had been a woman, reincarnated as Lady Frazer.
When she dies at a secret location
(Her official obituary having been published
Years before), the children of the children
Of the Personhood of the Golden Bough

Keep alive her memory in sibylline sayings,
Videos and verses that can be unscrambled
By initiates only, hidden in sacred groves,
Chanting in unison in an age when wow and flutter
Have utterly gone, in a marketable future
In countries whose frontiers have been sanitized
Against all subversive thinking, on a planet safe for
    nostalgia.
Where zoom lenses lie glutted on the crewcut grass
You can hear crackly chanting on bootleg tapes:

'She places live hummingbirds in the tubes for duty-free
    cigars.
She is not caught.'

'She carries rare seedlings in her moist spongebag.
She is not caught.'

'She picks the mortar out of retaining walls.
She is not caught.'

'She leads the wind, nourishing it, into the crevices
Of dry-stane dykes. She is not caught.'

'She forges visas. She is not caught.'

'She emerges fully-formed from the head of Zeus.
She is not caught.'

'God smuggles Christ into her womb.
She is not caught.'

'She treasures the customs of all the peoples.
She passes through customs, bearing the seed of the new.
She smuggles towards us as we wait for her by the shore.
She croons in Gaelic "I have nothing to declare." '

VIA

Two middle-aged Church of Scotland ministers
Hike the Makar's Glen in 1940.
The taller one trips into a burn
Up to his waist.
'Quit laughing, you beggar.'
Hauled out, he peels off dark serge trousers.
His friend wanders over the sheep-nibbled slope,
Comes back with bone-dry plus-fours;
But the droukit man just shakes his head;
Strides on in longjohns; conversations about bombing
And the congregation at Boquhan. 'Yon sun heat's
Drying me out.' Then the long tramp
Down from the summit, each with his stick:
My grandfather and my great uncle Campbell
Who wouldn't wear a scarecrow's trousers.

PRAYER

Upstream from shattered urban lintels
Lost crofts are soft as new bread.

That dripping tap in the one-walled kitchen
Reminds someone there will be a need
Of water before and after.

Sin to imagine a perfect world
Without embarrassment, rain, or prayer.
A hand is clasping my other hand

In a dark place that has to be got through
On a wing and. Listen to this.

WHA'S LIKE US?

Each night on the map of Scotland
He scored out a name: ~~Tanera Mor~~, ~~Oban~~,

And above each inked-over place he wrote
The name of a child who had died of starvation

In another part of the world:
~~Kirkcudbright~~, ~~Stromness~~, ~~Inverailort~~ . . .

Some nights more than one place disappeared,
Replaced by the foreign syllables

In a fountain-pen hand: ~~Ferguslie~~, ~~Inchinnan~~,
Until all of the mainland and islands

Were black with his script, and no native word
Was left on the map. You could not read

All the overlapping syllables of foreign children
Whose inked-in names when you stood at a distance

Formed the exact silhouette of Scotland.

BOY

My left hand is turning into a herring.
The fingers I write with get doughy

So it hurts to shake hands – feels as if
People tear at my fingers like rolls.

I want to greet them with my left. They shun it
Because it has a briny smell,

But out here in a strange place I'm learning
To cope with offering both hands

To the sitting crowd. When they grip me, each man and
      woman
Seems full. This

Must be the meaning of shaking hands
With five thousand people. They're rising,

Fed, leaving the bowl of the hills
Strewn with left-overs, me among them.

Everybody's gone now. I'm just thirteen.
I understand I don't understand it.

MC

'Going to hell in a hurry. Send *The Wykehamist*'.
1916, awarded Military Cross.

MA, BD. At Nakusp, BC,
Preaches to thumbless lumberjacks. Takes tea at Harvard.

New charge – galvanic Pope of Govan –
Unemployed and Iona Abbey

Rebuild one another as ordered.
World War Two: 'I am a man

With a jammed Bren gun, but not so jammed.
I hit with one bullet in five.'

Old age, psoriasis: put feet in poly bags.
Tell Duke of Edinburgh: BAN THE BOMB.

Immersion

In mud, weeds, leaves, preaching
Christ of Ecology at Morven, car converted

To diesel in the 70s. Public weeping when wife dies,
Wrinkles in the age of the image.

We Shall Rebuild. Iona rebuilt.
We Shall Rebuild. Yells: 'I have maintained

This single-minded passion for so many years
By being deaf.' Military. Cross.

SARAH

My husband's a bachle. I love him.
A hundred, his penis is a rag.

Listening to foreigners, I laughed at the tentflap.
He squints at me now, a nodding camel,
Dry lips suspicious with faith.

What should I do, a woman of ninety,
Squalling like a baby at this new mirage
Beyond the tent door, finding how
God has made me for laughter?

CHURCH

It is the day
When bicoastal US academics,
Writers and singers who divide their time
Between Sydney and Wales, dealers
In vintage Ferraris, DJs, and adpersons
Make their way to a windswept, whitewashed
Presbyterian church, to walk
Down its narrow aisle, between pews filled
With gaunt-boned women who have lost their children.
This ceremony does not have a name.

THE FIRST JUDGMENT

The eyes will be judged first
Before they can return to their bodies.

There's an enormous queue of them, a voice asking
Did you see on television

Poor people with captions in front
Explaining what they said in their dialects?

What did you video? When you went outside
Did you avert yourselves from anything odd?

The eyes look at each other. This

Isn't what they expected. They want to argue,
But they are no longer linked up to mouths.

They want to elect a brilliant spokesperson,
Without hands. They want

To be able to make various deferred gestures,
To wink, to authorize immediate payment,

To shut themselves tightly against the light.
But they have no bodies, no eyelids.

Eyes who watched television, and eyes who were watched
Stare at each other. Some of them burst into tears.

Others know that without tearducts
They are no longer able to cry.

Eyes who are crying, and dry, clear eyes
Examine one another intently.

Right, says the voice, you've been judged.

A CHANGE

As we drive, the firth beside us
Is turning to wine, and a local woman

Is dying of cancer.
This is a hard place

Where the seed fell among thistles
And grew in defiance. Through corrosive rain

While she is dying you can see the hillsides
Shine with their vineyards that do not exist:

O wines of Pittenweem, I sing your praises;
O Chateau Motherwell, O Chateau Dingwall,

Grape of the haar when everything transforms
And spins and rallies its kaleidoscope

Of village Canas and the end of life,
With dancers asking for a glass of water.

NEXT MOVE

for Les Murray

I saw a house once, built of clapboard,
Silent, going for a song.

Princeton University wanted it off its books
So had parked it on a lot behind the library

Where cats surveyed its non-foundations
Raised a bit off the ground.

All we had to pay were the transport fees:
$10,000 a mile.

I looked at its porch, its two tall storeys
Up in the air. We couldn't shift it a block,

But there it stood, free as America,
In move-in condition, rich.

How could that have crossed an ocean?
What would it have looked like in Glasgow?

Maybe somewhere a millionaire
Would have taken the risk. I made my right decision

Aware each step I took down the street
How much the next move would cost me.

The manse he grew up in had a big glebe where there was room for him to breed Shetland ponies. They would drive the ponies out from Aberdeen with the sheep from market. He never grew flowers, but when he went into the army in 1940 waiting at Chelsea Barracks before going to France he worked as a gardener. He would steal flowers from the gardens of abandoned rich people's houses and replant them around the nissan huts. He stood to attention with a shouldered spade when the General came to inspect. His Brigade of Scots Guards was commended for its well-kept grounds. He stayed there for a year, transplanting flowers through the bombing. It is all he talks about; not the time after at Normandy and north to the Baltic; not even the blackout, or bren-gun training, or tanks. Just the gardening. Men with less green fingers went through the camp faster and died. His spade saved him, and his intelligent thefts. After the war he kept digging, in Kent and in Scotland: brussels sprouts, strawberries, potatoes; delphiniums, white heather, tulips. If you look back through all he has done, more prominent than the Depression or the Second World War, than the Sixties or Thatcher will be this continuity of soil-covered fingers, trowels, roots and bulbs.

ABERDEENSHIRE

Oilrig excaliburs of burning gas,
Sheep coughing through a starlit igloo silence
Near Craigievar, the reeling of dancers

Spattering an on-off wind's signal
Broken up by granite and salmon,
Whitewater *bon viveurs*.

The King's College corona satellite-tracks
Star dialects. Hills budge
And settle. Grouse flurry. Computer screens dazzle the
   night,
Their flickering eyes added to the land's.

TECHNOLOGY TRANSFER

I know little about Scotland only Millport
I left when I was fourteen in the rain

To go to Queensland when I saw your photos
Of the house on Great Cumbrae I cried

Her voice
Gets ahead of itself, aware of small lace-up shoes

Left behind on the side of the world
Without aeroplanes or tv.

Her birthday predates that of plastic.
Her emigration is everybody's

Now to set out means being left behind
By more stylish technologies: ships called Personal
    Computer,

Carphone, Creditcard. We travel by manmade fibres
Towards a New World that is already

Dated or being upgraded,
Singing of the Old Country, its mangles and crystal sets,

A never-changing holiday continent
Of reel-to-reels, grubbers, 78s,

Where our great inventors wore shorts or pinnies
In the places from which we were cleared.

BOND

In his late eighties he still took his dog to the cinema. They went to see *You Only Live Twice*. His daughter-in-law would get very embarrassed; 'someone's got to sit on that seat afterwards.' Ears cocked, the collie perched on the velour. A man in the row behind leant forward, gave a tap on the shoulder. 'Hey, mister, is yur dug enjoyin the pictchur?' 'Aye, son, can ye no tell? He's seen all the James Bonds. He feels it's a shame it's no still Sean Connery but.'

THE HUMANITY CLASSROOM

Sitting there, I was a comma in the bible;
On either side great generations of talk.

The word means Latin. Stubbornly at the Uni
They went on calling it Humanity.

Before my time, in mid-*Aeneid*
A woman at the lectern under big oil portraits

Threw open a window, leaned out listening
To riveters at work in the shipyards.

ARTHUR E. MEIKLE

'Who's Mister Meikle?'
'Head English teacher.'

(Alasdair Gray, *Lanark*)

The lecturer who'd said the word 'English'
Stood urbanely, fitted his monocle
To his left eye, and slowly pirouetted
From east to west, his gaze going over the singers

Like a screen wiper.
Scissors snipped your Sherlock Holmes briar
From black card for a silhouette
That hangs in the study, eerily neat as your own

Italics before the stroke.
There is a line of boys in worn blazers
Walking towards you, passing through you, ghosts
Into Scotland's distance. You watch them, smiling

In a tenement room. You remember the future
In its home-made short trousers,
Silent, except when your wife says 'That
Was a long time ago,' you say, 'Aye.'

THE GLASGOW HERALD

On industrial evenings serenaded by welding
At Colville's Steelworks, one white-hot pouring arc
Glimpsed from a diesel, I carried my paintings in a plastic
  sack

Through Central Station, hearing the woman announcer
Calling Ardrossan, Polmadie, Haymarket, Pollokshaws, a
  random timetable
Rich as Los Angeles, New York with bracken and grass.

Her messages in the middle Sixties
Still held a departing tremor of steam, the Greenock
Blitz, torpedoes on wagons, my parents' threatened

Destinations. At Dalmarnock Power Station the sky
  enlarged
Over and over, above towerblocks, beyond the Campsies
Brushed by works hooters, the lyric blasts of a train.

AT LANSDOWNE KIRK

You see from gold-leaf behind the pulpit
Between the years 1914 and '19
McNeil was not a good name to have.

'*I am the true Vine.*' In plaster relief
Behind St Andrew, St Margaret, St Mungo
Are kneeling killers – Wallace, and Robert the Bruce

With the words 'Death or Liberty' at his ear.
The bare toes of Christ's right foot
Peep from his robe. Round him

The only figure in modern dress
Is a kilted solider, kneeling with fixed bayonet.
Seventy years after the Armistice

He is still holding, still laying down his gun.

GLASGOW 1989

for Frank Kuppner

Wind souchs on the hot lawns of Kelvinbridge.
Back after ten years, a young Sikh stares at where
   tenements were
In the early evening, remembering
How he grew up under this grass.

In the newsagent's/gapsite/demolished warehouse
Janice is xeroxing copyright music,
Singing *Flower of Scotland*. That ex-
Railway bridge is just sky.

A sculpted paper boat, berg-sized,
Floats off berths zoned for redevelopment.
Wee Shuggy, Dave, and Wonderwoman
Hang around waiting for a zebra.

FIANCÉE

She reads by gas. Their engagement will be as long
As her mother's illness. A motor car splashes on the
cobbles.

Each Christmas they exchange poets
In the padded leather bindings that will soon go out of
fashion.

She glides upstairs, carrying fresh linen.
Mother walks to the toilet. Clouds are banked over the
Firth.

In his photograph he is wearing a starched wing-collar.
They initial their endpapers, adding the date:

'07, '08, '09.
Upstairs is quiet. She sits in the parlour

Patiently reading, *'I am very dreary,*
He will not come', she said.

LOVE POEM FOR ALICE WITH OLD CARS

In the new dream I give you a big-radiatored
100-miles-on-a-gallon-of-water steamcar
Exported by the White Sewing Machine Co.,
Cleveland, Ohio. You scoot with aplomb

Through Alexandria to Loch Lomond past the indigenous
Argyll Motors Factory with its built-to-last
Stone car over the door. People call you odd,
Determined, unchaperoned, 'fast'. Your wheels cover

Scotland, familiar and intimate, Tin-Lizzying
Right up Ben Nevis, mass-produced,
Laughing with the dash of the woman driver's
TS1, first car in Dundee. Your fingers

Run through my hair in the rain with the uniqueness
Of Tullock's 1910 St Magnus
Handmade on mainland Orkney. A crowd of boys in caps
Skips beside us, mouthing

Names of shared loves: Arrol Johnston,
Delaunay-Belleville, Renault. A twine of exhaust
Ties up the Pass of Brander. Can the greenhouse effect
Scrub out this joyful woman driver

Insouciant at the wheel of a Detroit-built Hudson, her
    glance
Thrown devil-may-caringly through its rear window,
Male passenger, watching her high heel pushing eagerly
Up away into the hills?

ANNE OF GREEN GABLES

Short moneyless summers at West Kilbride you sat out
On the back steps with a view of the outside toilet
Reading the Anne books, one after the datestamped next,

Anne of Windy Willows, Anne of Avonlea,
Anne of the Island, Anne's House of Dreams.
No books were ever as good as these

From West Kilbride Public Library
That always had to go back.
When we got married, one by one

You bought the whole set, reading them though. At first
I was jealous when you sat not speaking,
Then put the books away on your own shelf.

' "How white the moonlight is tonight," said Anne
Blythe to herself.' At first
I was jealous. Not now.

ITERATION

It just won't stop, the solution of a simple equation
Fed in again at the start

Forever and ever in fractal geometry,
Producing a four-dimensional model

Of how things Topsy, cat's eyes on the ringroad,
A fern's replicated

Sameness of tracery, a fir tree's cone after cone.
We live among it, on a modern estate

With four Daves, five Bhattacharjyas. I don't want to
    move,
Just have it all happen, the nuisance of another day

Of childlessness, another day of being in love –
One water droplet, then four, the singular

That is also a plural, the true thing that always changes,
Greek Department and Microcomputer Suite

Alike called The Swallowgate, our marriage that is
Monday, Tuesday, Wednesday, Thursday,

Friday, Saturday, Sunday,
-day, -day, -day, -day, -day.

HOMMAGE

Tongues furred with unheard words, holts, eyes against a
   sheet of carbon.
She wears this, she strews it about her
In shirts and placenames, bras.

After, in the morning, across distant fields,
The linnet is wild about the linnet.

Shifting peat-banks, subsidences, elbows
Out of the water around her islands,
Remarkable natural arches

Or in the supermarket her ears and dark places
In touch with one another, secretly.

Her wiry hair, her singing, her ancestor the baker.
She is the beach and its spring tides. She is Loch Morar,
Scales and guitar-riffs. I put my ear to her belly:

The glut and knock of
Porpoise.

DIRECTOR

Random cars manoeuvre, oxygen
Bubbles up slowly through a glass of orange. A flypast
Doesn't happen. Soaking it all in
Filters out the undesirable
Without seeming to do so, like a tourist brochure
That slips from your fingers as you doze off in the canvas
    chair
With *Director* across its back.
This afternoon a radiographer
Locates the X-rays of someone dear to you
Taken twenty years ago, and matches them against
    Tuesday's.
She is beginning to dial her call
Right in the middle of your speculation
That phonewires reflected in Bell Street's windows
Are accidental artworks – the streetlife
Ditto, just for a sec, before you hear
About the dark patch pressing on a lung.

CONSUL

You were a stranger in Greenock at a Burns supper
The night the shipyards were axed.

'There are more statues of Robert Burns
In Australia than anywhere outside Scotland,'
You heard yourself saying. Then an ex-
Crane-driver sang 'Scots Wha Hae'.

You saw his wife, standing with an orange juice,
Saying nothing, dignified as a heron
At a polluted pool who can't understand
She'll see no fish there again.

NORTH-EAST FIFE

You are the instrument
Generations have played on

Under the fields of Crail and Anstruther
Combs and mirrors in an Aero-bar darkness

After the Picts, small stone churches
Outlived cathedrals as a tin whistle outlasts an organ

You are the true postmodern script
Whose every letter is robbed from an earlier writing,

Unkirkcaldied, Dundeeless, smug,
Too full of your earlier selves,

Sunlit evenings' bohemian fishertowns,
Home of the avant-golf,

In between the high-summer fields
Identities spilling like wisps of hay

Blown from the back of a horse-drawn cart
That is slowly becoming a tractor.

MARY SHELLEY ON BROUGHTY FERRY BEACH

One small boat tugs the enormous corpse inshore
Towards waiting locals. A lad opens up its mouth
And wades inside, clutching a flensing tool
For blubber. Piece by hacked-off piece

Men deconstruct the outcast zeppelin body,
Carting lumps back to beachfront cottages –
Sturdy food and good oil for the winter.
Harpoons glint in the candlelight.

Safe home, the men of Broughty Ferry take
Their sweet uncorseted wives to bed, or croon
Shanties to bairns beside toys made of teeth.
The Tay flows quiet. Dundee's lights wink their yellow.

A sad girl walks from the beach, carefully picking
Her steps as she sneaks past a leftover eye
Flung on the sand, and other small last bits
Of monster littering the promenade.

NAPIER'S BONES

Beyond St Andrews, out past Edenbellie,
You married and made love above the orchard
Of Gartnes Castle where the Endrick's cold

Incessant abacus of water plunged
Through a lint-mill opposite. Its *clack clack clack*
Forced you to yell to the miller on the other bank

To stop his wheel and let your thoughts flow free
Towards logarithms and Calvin's feuars' quarrels
Out at Boquhopple. Then you lost

Your first wife, buried her, and thought again.
Refinement of manures, and common salt,
Hydraulic force and constantly revolving

Axles obsessed you, clearing flooded pits
Throughout all Scotland. Grimly you refuted
God's foes with a battle tank, then, plagued by gout,

Invented Rabdiologiae, your ivory
Computer uttering through speaking rods
23025850, the world's

First calculator. Your eleven children
Would have to see this other, stranger child
Outlive them, accurate as today's pale sun

Wet above Helensburgh, shining on
Two sundials once at Gartnes Castle, buried
In an overgrown garden. Napier's bones.

ST ANDREWS

When you had finished, you replaced the beaches around the town, the Kinness Burn, and the surrounding fields. You put back the buildings on North Street, Market Street, and South Street exactly as you had found them. After taking apart St Salvator's spire stone by stone you reglazed the sky above it. You hadn't found God in masonry crevices or under mortar, but you were aware of Him in the act of deconstruction and reassembly. You did everything so perfectly, no one noticed any difference. A few people hesitated in the narrow streets as if arrested by an odd smell, maybe of dust, or of earth that had been built on for centuries then suddenly for a moment released to the air. Taxis came, laden with students and golfers. Bejants processed. The life of the town went on; it was years before things were seen to have altered. These changes can be linked to your name, now hailed as important. We took you on trust and you were grateful for that. We didn't ask too closely. Walking to my office I can see that the trees, the cobbles, the tenements and shopfronts, even the sea, have been lightly dusted with your attentive, paintless brush.

STEP-ROCK POOL

Rooky ur-stanes, nesh
Wi deid weans' haunprents, sclimmin
Salvatour's tooir. Toon
Blae wi rimaindird buiks, *Echoes*
an Re-echoes, A'm goannae mollocate
Yir fey wynds, goannae burstle
Yir douce stanes, goannae bigg
A New Toon
Fur ma kid's nesh fit, steppin in.

Misty stones of the beginning, delicate with the handprints
of dead children, climbing Salvator's tower. Town blue
with remaindered books, *Echoes and Re-echoes*, I'm going
to totally destroy your fey lanes, break up your respectable
stones, build a New Town for my child's delicate foot,
stepping in.

LORD PETER SPLITS A GUT

'Excuse me, sir, have you been drinking?'

'Why, yes, officer. I have just consumed
A bottle of the most excellent Napoleon brandy.
I was dining with my old friend, the Chief Constable.
We were up at Balliol together.'

'Stiff news, milord,' interrupts Hook of the *Daily Yell*,
'The mutant prawns are creeping again. Professor
    Lumsden's
Out there in his diving helmet. He says in an hour
They'll have broken through the eight-mile limit.'

'But the diamonds, man. Does he have the diamonds?
If only I'd known that Lady Boak was wearing them.'
It's deadly funny. There's a Labour Government. 'Bunter,
What does one wear to a Nirex plant in Dundee?'

THE CATALOGUE OF SHIPS

The Dundee Homeric Society appeals for sponsors,
Ignoring its own oral epic

Jammed out by jute-barons and soft-focus journos
Writing their PR *Dundoniad*

Through whose sieve the undiscovered
Pour down – a firth that shines like India,

Sharp as the Archangel snows –
Every person a kind of vessel

History does not list:
The dissector's cousin clenching her small leather bag

While the Ferry Road floods with elephant,
The unshod, the filthy-shoed, councillors coughing and
    nudging,

Arctic footballers, bridge rebuilders,
The Submarine Miners' Brass Band:

Everyone here is ordinary,
Silvery, hard-faced, bonnie.

HOSTILITIES

Accusing the D. C. Thomson group of continuing to hold the national mind intellectual hostage, the Scottish fleet has commenced its bombardment of Dundee.

Under the terms of the Treaty of Glenrothes, the islands of Rifkind and Little Forsyth are to revert to their former names.

Professor Helen Abercrombie, composer, assassin, and inventor of the Rat-Bomb, has been freed in an exchange of prisoners.

At the Glasgow School of Art an outbreak of typhoid has been traced to tinned produce carrying cooking instructions in Scots and Gaelic.

The pictorial calendar industry is to be nationalized, President Kelman announced yesterday.

Edinburgh has surrendered again.

DOING TELEVISION

I'm made up too. The anchor-person's face
Smiles along a plate-glass coffee table
Piled with closed books. It's like living

In a furniture showroom. 'OK, let's take
That last joke again, Robert.' Home
I start to wash the lacquer from my hair.

ILLNESS

Illness drives a new road through your life.
You lie beside its cars and trucks.

It has its own quiet spells, rush-hours,
Buzzing where there were fields.

Everyone in the cars looks fit and well
As they speed towards the reshaped horizon,

But exhaust leaks from village-sized lorries,
Making you cough, shortening your sentences

To a few words. Tail-lights wink in the dark.
One moment you see them, then the next.

KILLER

Onscreen Hannay and Mr Toad
In an aquascutum, chased in expensive cars
All through the Tokyo figures
Down on last night's. Our eight clocks
Show morning somewhere, all the time
A new market opening up.

Lenin's Tomb without Lenin. Moving
To a market economy. 50m
Through Tokyo again at dawn.

You may picture me driving that 40 h.p. car for all she
was worth over the crisp moor roads on that shining May
morning (I made a killing); glancing back at first over my
shoulder, and looking anxiously to the next turning (we
wiped them out); then driving with a vague eye, just wide
enough awake to keep on the highway (I got a real buzz,
could smell the money). For I was thinking desperately of
what I had found in Scudder's pocket-book.

Onscreen, faces, mine
Weaselly, reflected in theirs
Looking at me through the screen, figures
Just bone, and babies
Gone when Tokyo opened.

When I logged on I felt lucky. Sammy
Knew all my signals – Ratty, Sir Walter Bullivant,
Marmaduke Jopley, Toad Hall.
We made a killing, thought
It was fine, in that light
With no windows, that dry light,
No weather, no morning, no nights.

Tiny door in the Wild Wood, in the snow, scraping, in the
   snow
Covering up the way in to safety, scraping and scraping to
   that small brass plate like a screen
I need to see, neatly engraved in square capitals. New
   figures coming onscreen.

Christ. We lost millions. The shredders. Christ.
YOUR PASSWORD IS INCORRECT

A WEE SEAT

You need more time to think it all out,
So much glass in the world.

Hours hunting for wallpaper to match,
Not finding it. And meetings,

Days of agendas, minutes.
Then your brother died.

Phone off the hook; sabbatical
You told everybody, sitting down,

Staring through the (rude word) window
Just as if it wasn't there.

SKELETON

The VDU reflects their froggy eyeballs
Peering in.

'Monday or Tuesday was it?' 'I'm not sure.'
'We've had so much on in the changeover period, the

Final audit.' Text floods over the screen;
See if I don't, ya cunts, ya

Motherfuckers. 'Anyway, we'll need to advertize
Discreetly.' 'Yes, Monday or Tuesday.

He filled his filing cabinet with sand.'

MARX

Harpo's scissors snipped the tails
From the ambassador's morningdress and disembowelled
A philosopher's enormous beard.

Orchids wept tapwater into people's eyes;
Buttonholes winked as an aristocrat who fell
From the roofgarden trampolined to safety.

Afterwards, ads for coffee, semolina,
And scouring powder. Harpo's best trick yet.
Father was dying upstairs.

ORAL

You taste salt spray and the day changes,
A boiled sweet, licked
From grey to opal to another colour
You're trying to name. Impatient as champagne

You can't but you want to – on the tip of your tongue,
    like forgetting
The next verse at yon Burns Supper, confident
It still belonged to you, and would tomorrow
When you'd slept with the taste of the toasts;

Or like that French test where you'd spit out
The Greek for it and the English, then veer off,
Correct at the wrong moment.
You knew later what you wanted to say, rolling

Names round your mouth till you got high on them –
O-ral Rob-erts U-ni-versity – you'd think about girls and
    their lips,
Practice whistling or mouthing under your breath
ὁ ἡ τό, τόν τήν τό, τοῦ τῆς τοῦ, τῷ τῇ τῷ, proud

To know the Greek for 'the' and be carrying
Homer from school in your bag, going back
To dad in his worn chair by the phone
With his mouth open, snoring

Before he woke up sharply, almost choking
When he started, as miraculously
As the baby you'd been, lying there, watching,
Swallowing, beginning to talk.

The FORWARD PRESS

Top 100 poets

of the YEAR

VOLUME I

One of the most influential poetry releases of 1999

Edited by IAN WALTON

First published in Great Britain in 1999 by
FORWARD PRESS LTD.
1-2 Wainman Road, Woodston,
Peterborough, PE2 7BU
Telephone (01733) 230759

SB ISBN 1 86161 590 6

FOREWORD

One thing, I had never done was to 'judge' a poetry competition ... it was with a great deal of trepidation I approached the task.

MANY YEARS AGO; ten to be precise, I opened an envelope and extracted a cheque for £150. At the time I was, like most poets, penniless and wondering where the next SAE for the return of my work would come from.

I did a double-take before realising that I had won 1st prize in an international poetry competition. I made the usual promises: I will not cash the cheque; I will frame it; I will cherish it; etc. However, reality ruled the day and I promptly paid the money into my bank account.

The years have passed and during that time I have been deeply involved in publishing; printing and promoting poetry, editing books, magazines and journals, and conducting workshops from Watford to Whitemoor prison. One thing, until last year, I had never done was to 'judge' a poetry competition.

As I feel that judgement and poetry should not really occupy the same sentence it was with a great deal of trepidation I approached the task.

During the course of the year 'Forward Press', through its various and diverse imprints, had agreed to publish just over 32,000 poems. The editors, and assistant editors, had been collecting, selecting, and surreptitiously secreting the poems that, in some way, had particularly moved them.

At the beginning of Oct 98 I was presented with almost two thousand poems from which to select the final 100 poets who would, as I had done, open an envelope and extract that elusive cheque.

The stakes this time were somewhat higher: I was charged with the responsibility of awarding £3,000 to the 'winner', £500 to the two 'runners-up', four prizes of £250, ten of £100 each, and a further 83 prizes of £50. £10,000 in total, and an awesome task.

This task, for an adjudicator, is exacerbated by the fact that a poem that has appeal on a Monday morning can lose it on a Friday afternoon: the selection can be influenced by the emotional state of the judge at the time they read the poems.

So what won, how, and *why?*

When selecting poetry for publication I have my own system. Firstly, the last thing I want to know is the name of the author so this is obliterated. Secondly, I look for a trinity; (believing all things have their own) and with poetry it is content; form; and spirit. On first reading, any poem that I felt filled any of the above three criteria made its way to the 'next pile'. The others, unfortunately were discarded, but only after a second reading a day or two later. The remainder were again subjected to the same scrutiny. Content: the actual words used, the similes, the metaphors. Was every word needed? Did the words used match the subject matter? Did it *sound* like the voice of the poet? Form: whether traditional verse or free verse, was there a rhythm? Did the thread carry from the first syllable of the title to the last syllable of the last line? Did the poem *feel* right? Then, spirit: the inexplicable element that Dylan Thomas described so well (or not so well) - 'poetry is what makes my toes tingle'. So at this point a poem with two of the three elements went through, which actually, thank goodness, meant the 'Top 100' had almost selected itself.

spirit: the inexplicable element that Dylan Thomas described so well (or not so well) - 'poetry is what makes my toes tingle'.

At this point in a competition an outside influence invades the process: - there has to be a degree of personal preference although one will try to be impartial. I tried to be impartial and ended up with my short-list of the required seventeen poems.

It is now, if reading this, that the eighty-three poets who received fifty pounds can take some solace: another judge, another competition, maybe a different short-list, such are the vagaries and I make no apology for my selection.

I paced the office for many hours, shuffling and re-shuffling the pack to whittle down to the last seven and wrote '£100 winner' on ten poems with a heavy heart. Seven remained and the collective editorial staff of 'Forward Press' harangued me as to who they were and lobbied vociferously (and even threatened) to try to influence the final decision. However, with no disrespect to Andrew Button: a marvellous poem that inspires from the very title (all too often overlooked by writers), and then the visual imagery of the first three lines when I actually held my breath waiting for the fourth -

J C Fearnley: maybe the subject matter was too ingrained in my own gallivanting memory, fine traditional verse with no archaic slip-ups -

Paddy Lease: his 'Diana' poem - one of over five thousand we received - said it all and if the job of 'Poet Laureate' is to write on subjects of 'national importance' then maybe Paddy should get the job.

Valerie Leith: short, succinct, to the point - not a wasted word.

All four poems, wonderful in their way but destined for only £250 each.

Last three - more hours of anxious pacing.

Maybe, and just a thought, Roger Taber and Susie Barker were too personal. Maybe I balked at such reality. The first line - along with the title '1982' of Susie's poem brought a tear to my eye - and still does each time I read it. I could not seriously send £3,000 to someone who made me cry - and Roger Taber, perhaps his poem - (one of many) is too arm-twisting, it is difficult to face our own prejudices no matter how open-minded we feel we are.

So that is why neither Susie or Roger won the first prize - why did Sally Spedding?

Well, my belief is that novelists are failed poets and Sally accomplishes in thirty lines what other writers take three hundred pages to achieve. The first four and a half lines - I am with the guy; with the cowhand, then she drops in the contrast - *and his*

My belief is that novelists are failed poets ... Sally accomplishes in thirty lines what other writers take three hundred pages to achieve.

cow/heavy with milk. What, I thought, could be more important to this cowhand. What had moved him?

Then I felt, as he did, panic - sheer panic. Perhaps the 'Titanic' bug was still in me, perhaps I am just a sentimentalist at heart; perhaps someone I loved did not buy a £1 Sun ticket for the Herald of Free Enterprise -

enough - enough - just read, slowly and feel -

Ian Walt

Ian Walton

Nothing has given me more pleasure in recent years than signing those one hundred cheques, but it's six months on, and still I worry if my choice was right.

CONTENTS

Cowhand

Through the muck he ran.
Soft dung pats sucking
His rubber calves
To that wide mirror
Of sky grey water. And his cow
Heavy with milk.
He'd seen the pretty toy town train
All lit up
Fall like a dying firework
Into the threshing flood.
He pulled again. Uncomprehending,
Calling his lover's name,
Rhiannon. Who gives the living sleep.
But now too deep
To take the dead.
Small window corner above the torrent.
Frail. Man-made
A flimsy tomb
For those who'd paid half price
For the pleasure
Of its cold embrace.
A best night-dress folded
Round a pouch
Of lavender.
Fish food. Out of reach
To the propellered flock above
Scouring the shadows.
Hovering. Stirring his hair
And haunting at night
His slurried sleep.

Sally Spedding

1982

And where was God today? Not here with us,
The devastating noise and then -
The silence it evoked - before the rush of
Agonising screams, the dreadful sounds,
Of people sighing, moaning, crying, bleeding,
Dying, their bodies wracked in pain, mutilated,
Limbs torn from them, - Christ -
These bloodied jumbled heaps of lifeless rag,
A large and unsolved human jigsaw, crushed,
Fragmented in this cruel and graceless grave,
Happy in their separate ways, a minute past,
And where was God today? Not here with us!

And where was God today? Not here with us,
With aching heart and trembling hand I knelt
To help, in what small way, I, useless could!
A choking layer of dust had filled our lungs,
The smoke and flames grew nearer, yet more close,
And all the doctors, nurses and police,
Were working fast,
A woman close at hand, said - 'do not fret -
It is God's way' - I choked within,
Clenched my fist, bit on dust - but
Could not say - and
Where was God today - not here with us.

Susie Barker

Ordinary People

Yesterday, we came to tell the world we're here
But the world we looked for wasn't there
So we took out a joint mortgage
On another planet, of lengthening shadows
By day, cosy silences
By night. All earthy modernity
Taken fright of two very ordinary people
Whose clothes, hair, ears, eyes
Would have taken no-one by surprise
But, rather, we'd have liked to hear it said
By more faces in glad places
While there was still time

See those two? They're friends of mine

We tried to pretend it didn't matter
Because we had each other; but now
You're gone, dear friend, I stand alone
Against the tide of bitter sympathy
That threatens, just as it
Always did, you and I, for all
That we were two very ordinary people
Braving the same mud, sky
As any other pair in love
So twists of wire
That heap our grave
Conspire to show

See him? His friend was gay, you know

Roger Taber

A Dart Thrown

In that small pocket of pregnant time
between the throwing of the dart,
and the resounding thud of metal in bristle;
beds of breathing babies have been born,
funerals of fatalities gravely registered,
churches of couples have taken their vows
while courts of others have cast them aside.

During that graceful trajectory of flight
when the final outcome is still uncertain;
lunches of lucrative deals have been secured,
streets of small boys have fallen off their bikes,
races of religious wars have divided nations,
schools of Sarahs have achieved 4 As at A Level
while queues of Johns signed on for the first time.

In the charged moment of congested tension
when his opponent considers the margins of error;
one of only 16 remaining pits has already closed,
pulses of patients awoke to a new heartbeat,
unisons of unions have gone on strike again,
papers of peace may have been signed in Northern
    Ireland
while overdoses of addicts have tragically expired.

During that suspended ecstasy of flight
as we follow the fateful arc
of that dart's final, prized location,
more important journeys will never reach
Such a simple destination.

Andrew Button

The Taxi-Dancer

Her skin was like ivory, yet soft and warm.
    Her eyes, black with kohl, seemed as deep as a well;
Entranced by the grace of her delicate form
    I could not decipher the tales they might tell.

Her hair, hung behind in a long lustrous braid,
    Was subtly perfumed, and her tip-tilted glance
Made me long to caress her, but I was afraid
    For the rule was 'no contact' but during the dance.

A transient among an inscrutable race
    Each evening for just a few dollars Malay
I held her within my perspiring embrace
    As close as I dared, and the world went away.

Bereft of my senses when holding her near
    The promises made as we traversed the floor
I now blush to recall, though with hindsight I fear
    That nothing was said she had not heard before.

All too soon sent up country, where dreams faded fast;
    Girls wore black pyjamas and carried a gun.
My first brief encounter was almost my last
    And I knew the enchantment was over and done.

J C Fearnley

Blame

It wasn't me, said the paparazzi,
Shutters clicking,
Flapping in to catch the picture,
Make the millions,
Loud abusive and persistent,
Vultures on their prey.

It wasn't me, said the editors,
Chasing circulation figures,
All condemning paparazzi,
Buying pictures,
Showing close-ups,
Blurred beyond all recognition,
Fat cats out of sight.

It wasn't me, said the owners
Sanctioning and giving orders
Just fulfilling their agendas
Satisfying public intrest
Safely bolstered by their power
Unrepentant in the backlash
Full of pious cant.

It wasn't me, said the Family,
Strangling in their protocol,
Ostracising, agonising,
Failing in their understanding,
Trapped in a well-meaning muddle,
Cushioned from reality,
In their castles of despair.

It wasn't me said the chauffeur,
Vilified beyond description,
I just followed
Given orders,
Turned from hero into villain,
Scapegoat made to take the blame.

It wasn't me, said the Princess,
Reaching out to touch the heartstrings
Of the sad and aching people
Who mirrored her despair,
Seeking frantically for solace,
Building tragedy relentlessly,
As the adoration grew.

It wasn't me, said the public,
Unrelenting in their interest,
Grabbing juicy
Bits of gossip,
Justifying tabloid claims,
Seeking to devour the princess,
They had taken for their queen.

But above all, without question,
Guilty though they all may be,
I am sure because I must be,
It was not me,
Not me,
Not me.

Paddy Lease

Envy

Unaware of me
You walk, bump proud
Down every street.
Your toddler like gait shouts vulnerability,
And society responds.
Cradling you in gentle expectation
Of the child to come.

I too,
Once bore
That awesome power,
To captivate, gravitate to earth mother.
But failed society's expectations
By delivering a stillborn child.
And those who had worshipped at the shrine of
pregnancy
Shunned me.

Valerie M Leith

Dance Macabre (Progressive)

(Longmoor Camp 1952)

The clean cooking tins
Are stacked on my left,
No dirties remain to my right.
I relax, and ponder.

The water in the sink
Is tepid, greasy, grey
Leaving wrinkled bands on my arms.
I'll be no hero
In my short Army career,
Unlike others of
My year's call-up
Who are fighting in Korea
Or hostile jungles
Of Malaya.

But surely the war ended
Seven years ago?

'The Unspeakable Hun'
Is a good friend, soon to be
A loyal comrade.
On the other hand
Our 'Gallant Russian Ally'
Is to be hated,
Distrusted and feared.

Like some grim progressive dance
The war continues,
But we've all changed partners.

B R Edwards

The Egyptian Girl On Crete

The Egyptian girl is hitching from beach to beach.
Such a handsome face. Wrinkled black hair. A miracle
of emancipation, she assaults bare-legged each
   conservative hamlet.

Old women scowl behind distaffs but their grandsons
tighten a noose of chairs around this elusive goddess
in a cool bar betrayed by crates of fizz bottles.
They do not touch. They adore at close quarters.
'What is your name?' 'Where are you from?'
'My name is Charmian. I am Egyptian but I live in Paris.'
'You are beautiful. Will you marry me?'

Her companion Jacqueline sulks in accustomed
   isolation.

At sunset Charmian wades the clean sands of
   Falasarna,
scrutinised by Germans from tent and cavern.
'Are you alone?' 'My friend is coming.'
'You sleep here?' 'We're camping.' 'Where?' 'I don't
   remember.'

At sunrise she swims naked near the sign: *No Nudism.*
She dries herself slowly. The breeze snatches her towel
concealing, revealing brown breast and thigh.
The landworker, who kissed the priest's hand
watches furtively, concealed by an olive tree.
The vision of her body will torment him nightly.
He will ravish her though she is a thousand miles distant.

Already she is leaving. 'We are flying to Geneva.
Oh! I have a thorn in my foot.' But it is Jacqueline
   who winces,
presuming another artifice to gain attention.

I buy them drinks in the village. Jacqueline says,
    'Thank you.'
But Charmian is bullying a cowed truck-driver.
'Take us to Khania, alright then, Kastelli.'
She mounts the truck. She stands like a commander.

I am abandoned with the wounded in the dust of her
    chariot.

Peter Gillott

Rape Of Love

I have got to move away, Mike.
Don't look at me with such surprise.
I longed for gentleness in our loving
to give that ethereal feeling of ecstasy
that should be mine - it never happened.
An inflated life-size doll - I am not.
My soul was yours from the start,
this body joyously awaited your smooth invasion,
so great was my love for you.
But you failed me - in your haste.
My breasts were not miniature punch bags
to be prodded, slapped, nipped and bitten.
And Mike - bulldozer tactics were never required
to gain entry to my southern region.
Learn the difference between love and lust.
I cannot be your teacher, my dear.
True love is more an instinct than
curriculum study. Please understand, I must go.
If only to give you some time
for easing up with space to absorb
what loving entails. Firing on all cylinders -
waste of energy, slow down -don't race.
This fragile heart I leave with you,
be careful - it can break so easily.
There is much you can reflect on.
If you understand this message of mine,
find me when the timing is right.
But for now - I must get away.

Lil Joseph

Therapy

Their talking cure
didn't really help.
The fifty minute hour
which she spent listening
simply amplified her silence.
His definition of her problem
confounded her further.
With no solace presented
the treatment merely sealed the gash,
hid the wounds from vision.
A sticking plaster
of the cheap and nasty variety
which comes off at first contact
with water, and floats away
leaving the incision exposed
raw, susceptible to decay
from within.

Deirdre McMahon

4th **prize** winner

Love And Death

My mother held me very close,
beneath the green and silky eiderdown.
And we would hide from the heaving light
of wildly burning fires above.
She would try to pass away the time
and speak to me of love and death
and all that lies between.

She'd sometimes glimpse the sight
of clean and flowering fields of peace.
And tell me of the flush of pleasure
to feast upon ice cream.
She'd speak of lush exotic fruits
I'd only ever seen in books
and in my head in restive dream.

She'd place her hands about my ears
to muffle the scream of falling bombs.
And I'd taste her tears upon my lips
when I kissed her trembling cheek.
And then she'd pass away the time
and speak again of love and death
and all that lies between.

Now, she doesn't seem to know my name,
but I sometimes hear a loving word
upon her silent breath.
So I try to pass away the time
and speak to her of where she's been.
But she never mentions love nor death
and nothing lies between.

John Merritt

Lisle Stockings

I remember
My mother wore lisle stockings
In wintertime.
New,
Their colour was like strong tea
Stirred up with condensed milk.
Suspenders
Hung
From the buttress of her pink corset
And buttoned through her stocking tops
Held them close against her curvy legs
All-day-long.
At night though
They lay over the bedroom chair back
Limp as a puppet's legs,
Until upstairs draughts
Nudged the feet
Into a pantomime of nonchalance
As the candle flame bobbed and fizzed.

On Christmas morning,
One of her old lisle stockings
Was poky with presents for me.
A tangerine, wrapped in silver paper,
Bulged behind
The latticed darnings of the toe-line.
But, I remember remembering
When that stocking was new,
Its colour like strong tea
Stirred up with condensed milk.

Betty Morgan

The Guilt Of A Deadline

You ask me how I felt
when I woke, cold and sweating
at 3am on that Tuesday morning

when I stood and watched the
rolling clouds, the flame and dust
and vomit and disease;

you ask me how the dread
fell deep from in my throat
and writhed inside my stomach

as the cars danced in the streets
in skirts of rust and glass
and the days cried their injustices;

I told you it was shame,
a deeper red than the
Sacred Heart (now a ghost behind my eyes)

and how I drank and smoked
and laughed as a thousand men
burned, then set the world on fire

Happy new year,
war is here.

Kieran Quirke

The Poverty Trap

I see a band of pale-faced
and weary men all dwindled down
by days increasing in their weight.
No sustenance, no dwelling place
for generosity is rare.
I watch them brooding over death
or living still in charity.
I'm waiting for their hearts to break
as, sick in soul and body both,
they pray for immortality
because my name is Poverty.

I kneel beside an ancient crone
who stays alive through strength of will.
She mumbles twixt her toothless gums
until two icy lips are still.
As vultures glide above their prey,
I swoop on unprotected men
who sink into oblivion
or cease to care until they die.
They know that all their lives will be
forever in my cunning trap
because my name is Poverty.

Her spotless steps are scrubbed each day..
Imperfect clothes are darned and patched.
She manages to find a way
to pay her bills. I take a look
into her eyes and see the pride
still gleaming there, refusing help.
I know I cannot break her will,
as children scamper in the dirt
or laugh with untold happiness
until they learn subservience,
because my name is Poverty.

Nancy Reeves

I Cannot

I cannot contain this dried up drone
that threatens to explode!
Should I curl my tongue around some words
and let my thoughts be exposed?
Maybe . . .
I can scratch one from my head,
pretend I'm playing with my hair,
pick letters from each strand
and speak by hand, on paper, or blow air.

Lawrance Richards

Vacant Steps

She walked along the road
Every day of the year
A little dog by her side.
She carried her shopping -
Enough for one,
And some food for her dog.
I often watched her progress,
Slow as it was,
Until she disappeared
Around the corner.
She held her head down
But she saw me
Once -
And smiled . . .
Until
One day
She didn't come down the road;
'Taken to hospital,'
The neighbourhood gossips proclaimed,
'Died in her sleep, poor love.'
And then they forgot
Her and her dog
And it seems only me
And the pavement
Miss their steps.

Clare Waterfield

Ghost Dancers

they move confidently to riotous music
in mystic union to the rhythm of the dance.
hot, elusive masks sway
untouchable, like dreams
in a mysterious merging of self and crowd.

his dazzled thoughts escape
to embrace a black pirouette
face painted white
fine, soft hair brushing against his cheek.

the band is playing feverishly.
garish lights flicker.
he surrenders to her spell
intoxicated
fast, and faster in ecstatic dance.

when ashen light sneaks in
the music flags.
they stand on the dance floor
still close, breathless, fading.

somewhere a door bangs.
a glass breaks.
a titter of laughter dies away
mixed with the angry, hurried noise
of a motor car starting up.

a clear and merry peal of laughter rings out
eerie, shadowy
made of crystal and ice
bright and radiant
but hauntingly cold and inexorable.

doors open, cold air pours in.
the dancers, on fire a moment ago
shiver.
look at each other
strangers.

Alfa

Twilight Zone

yes, she has simply put her soul on ice
a soul usually taut and juicy
has shrivelled up
barren from constant giving
hot and feverish

now, red devils dance for her
choking her
mocking, bawling, destroying
won't let go
pushing fear to its limit
until she screams, spits
and her body stiffens

trapped wings flutter
against crippling tiredness
she lies awake in the chaos of the night
languidly, hopelessly searching
for an answer
waiting for the twilight of the gods

Alfa

Crossing The Border

A wake at night
Walking solemnly through
Monaghan town.
The chip shop
Turns its lights off
As the procession passes by.
I have no way
Of showing respect:
No blinds to pull,
No hat to doff;
I just stare and wait
For the traffic to clear,
Not wanting to look
Like a stranger here.

Roger Adams

Whispers

A whispering breeze speaks, rustling leaves with
gentle, bated breath
as solemn-toned hushed words inform of tragedy and
death.
Vile gossips' lies, maliciously, are spread to eager ears
as lovers' murmurs, passionate, engulf, inducing tears.

An indiscreetly mumbled hint, embellished, brings
disgrace
and harsh words silently are spat, foul-mouthed, at
distraught face.
With secrets shared by only two now brought to light
of day,
those hands that shielded wagging tongues
emphatically flay.

The trouble-mongers drift away, the thrill of chase
now gone;
with kill accomplished, whispering no longer lingers on.
But, what of prey they hunted, left mentally confused
when cornered by that baying mob and verbally abused?

Distress chokes words, unspoken thoughts lie heavily
within,
and muted anguish pounds away with undiminished din.
The acid bitterness of doubt burns fierce till thoughts
are blind,
all sensibility consumed by whispers of the mind.

An eerie silence fills the air, as sky - once bright -
turns grey,
enveloping surroundings in a monochrome array.
The gentle breeze increases strength, strong gusts
bring turbulence
and gales wreak havoc in their wake with fierce
malevolence.

Maureen Atkin

Inhaled

Sat in ritualistic circle,
Smoking memories,
Choking kisses,
Invoking numbness,
Melting into the soft space
Between consciousness
And unconsciousness,
Dislocated narcosis,
Somnambulistic sloth,
Slow time passed quickly,
We sucked life from it
And it sucked life.

David Atkinson

Rooms

I had room for you
so much space to fill.
You had rooms for me
in small hotels and
flats of friends.
In secret you made
space for me.
But your room was occupied.

L J Atterbury

Bedsit

The light bulb's
forty watt and naked
does its best to endear
but fails miserably,
like the last tenant.
Hope doesn't exist here
only sounds
the lonely footfall above
below:
the usual row.
Somewhere
a cry from a nightmare.
Trying to grab some kip
at least shows initiative
the flies of course
never do
doing the dance of death
around that damn light bulb
like a gibbet it is.
As I gaze up
from my damp mattress
the man above hesitates
his door slams
the row stops
Someone comes to
they all know
what I know
but we never show we know
when we say hello
every damned morning.

Gary Austin

5th winner

The Poppies' Pain

Blood red, a painful pun.

The wilted flowers lay pathetically
amongst the obliterated tablets of stone.
Memories clinging to the eroded petals,
death lingering sombrely.

Stuck in a rut of remembrance
poppies scream pain of long ago,
aspired to be a rising,
but was another falling.
The war to end all wars,
but didn't.

Youths in their prime ate dirt
shrouded in blood red analepsis,
in the faithful one's hearts.

Captive of the Green Fields.
Wear your Poppy with pride,
for that's all that remains.

Gemma Bowen

Untitled

I own only one thing
My aloneness
In the brown stream
Of my childhood
I watched the stickleback
I followed the stream
'Til it became a river
That's how I came to the city
Where everybody went around
With a whisker
That transmitted the constant din
Property Of So And So
Do Not Remove
I received all this
Down my own whisker
So I tried to bleep
Something about the stickleback
But it was no use
My aloneness
Became loneliness
And my mouth fled
To the tips of my fingers
There was only the racket
And the horrible idea
That I should have wandered
Upstream instead
Except
I had the idea for some fun
That I could swap
What I owned
With that of someone else
Easy
I have left the city now
And approach the sea

Perhaps one day to surf
The endless undulating wave
Of cries
The moans and sighs by night
That signal the intelligence
Desire comes unlooked for
At the last

Malcolm Bell

Winter Sailing Dinghies

Like fistfuls of white doves
(Their wings stiffened skywards,
Tensioned as feathers flick
Against breasted energy,
Straining talons) the sails
Cluster and jostle on the sea ramp
Preparing to race.
Look closely as they peel away
Horizontally separating one from the other
To discrete laminas: they're
Translucent or opaque - some

Diaphanous and veined as dragonflies
With corresponding crews
Of lean men: insects in rubber tubes -
Totally sheathed in black and colour -
Borne on bravado, wading chest high:
Iced water heroes
Rakishly nosing craft windward.
Ubiquitous plastics prevail:
Rainbow-coloured sheets to every part,
Outriggers and geodesic rudder-mounts,
Tiller extensions universally jointed,

A spinnaker pot that's not for prawns.
Odd-balls are there: latter-day misfits,
Mechanisms spare and skippers bearded,
In plywood hulls cross-grained and lacquered
As royal yachts once were -
Their love deep in the wood with
Trainer-shod college girls, buoyancy-aided,
Fresh and plump in 'Frisky' - as
Unconcerned as climbers
Roped to their destiny;
And all put out to the line:

To stewards in stuttering outboards -
Taking their chances, equally fragile,
With weather, wind, the wake of ferries,
With clawing undertows and tides -
Eccentric currents imperfectly predicted:
With Neptune intolerantly rising
To catch with his trident
The laggards or leaders,
The handicapped or hopeful -
Taking his pick
Of the boldest and most succulent.

F Bramah

Memories Of India

Delhi mid-morning, and dense human
traffic is alive with the thread of talk.
Porters bent double, under bales of
coloured silks, move with winged feet.

Markets entice with exotic fruit and spices.
Vivid scents compete with urinal stench,
human sweat and rotting vegetables.

Beggars, deep worn in years seek alms
from weary tourists who stare with
emotional mists in their eyes.

So many faces, so many castes, where
everyone's pain has a different smell, and
life's salt oozes out of every pore.
The scampering life of India moves onward.

Alexander Branthwaite

Humility

Humility. Your hand of discipline
falls heavy on my heart, and reaching in
to crush my pride and wither all my dreams,
reveals my poverty, until it seems
that I'm composed of little else but sin.

Of course, I set up my protesting din
and cower from Your Spirit's searching beams,
recoiling from the wisdom that esteems
humility.

I won't refuse this bitter medicine;
Your ruthless love, as sharp as any pin
has heard my prayer for fruitfulness, and deems
the humus as essential as the streams.
This is the soil where growing must begin:
humility.

Ros Bunney

Main Drag Pubs

Weekly this sorry procession
rolls out a parade of wannabe
kings and queens,
heirs unapparent to the realms of nothingness.

Girls with elaborate hairdos,
boys drenched in cheap cologne;
drawn to the main drag pubs,
solitary ventilators of the monochrome kingdom.

Factory gates closed, chained, padlocked;
the great Friday escape, a weekend parole
till Monday morning cracks a brutal dawn
of hangovers and regret.

Girlish expectation of that certain special
someone to sweep them
up in the arms of romance, die
as dead as stone at the first drunken leer.

Boyish dreams of page three sex kittens
doubling as wives to come home to;
dreams which exponentially dissolve with the
gradual expansion of nurtured beer guts.

Doomed to this since the rude
prime spark of conception;
but when there is next to nothing
embracing what there is becomes the only thing to do.

Girls grow shrill and dowdy,
hairdos architectural disasters,
age and sucking filter tips trace
sallow lines about lipstick-smeared mouths.

Boys grow fat and ape-like,
bitter shirt-bursting bellies barely
defying gravity, secreting peptic ulcers
swiftly germinating to perforation point.

Dreams drained of value, are clear no more,
lost in nicotine clouds and beer spills;
nothing remains save senselessness and habit,
still drawn to the main drag pubs.

All they wanted was a life,
not too much to ask;
but the main drag pubs are all there is
and happiness was never their promise to keep.

Tony Bush

5th prize winner

The Real Spirit

In the dog-eared photograph
three elderly women, seated,
hold plastic mugs aloft
in a concerted celebration.

They really don't look as if
they've got that much
to outwardly smile about
in this insipid setting
of care home decor
with its anaemic wallpaper
and Spartan furnishings
in a colour scheme for the dying.

Despite the mental resignation,
the physical discomforts,
and the social sidelining,
the obstinate presence
of their human spirit
squats in this picture
like a photogenic ghost
with its tongue sticking out.

Of course, it could just be
that the alcoholic elixir,
already drained from their mugs,
is starting to take effect.

Andrew Button

The Plastic Grin

Did she wheel this pushchair
around all the shops in town?
Did she get the same furtive glances,
the same wild, runaway curiosity
that I try to rein in, now?

Her stare is direct and unwavering,
I can see no disturbing subplot
behind the main story of her questions.
There is nothing in her polite manner
to suggest a snag in the fabric of her mind.

She exchanges pleasantries with me
as she would recipes with a friend.
Even in the nature of her subject request:
Health and Diet, I can imagine
little scope for a deranged agenda.

It's just the pushchair and its contents.
The small baby silent and motionless
with a face so flawlessly smooth
set forever in a plastic grin.

Andrew Button

Robot Man

A set of words fall together
And hit the bottom of my head
As hard as a brick
A useless attempt
At romance

The image is sickly
Traditional or complete
It is impossible
And thoughts choke
My impulse

Colleagues encourage and cajole
But my head is not responding
To their words or my feelings
The banging continues
I can't translate

John Carmody

The Celtic Prince

The city in summer encases me,
Chokes me,
With claustrophobic chaos.
That's when,
Dressed in robes of velvet green,
The Celtic Prince calls.
Across the sea he sits and waits;
My soul's ancient lover.
Here, in the dirt and the smoke,
His stories speak to me.
But only there, can I freely dance
Along orange and red embroidery
Of his gown's flowing hem.
Or roll through the Connemaran curves
Of his slender fingers,
And watch his cousin, the sun
Flicker over the western sea.
From here, I can hear his cries of pain
Inflicted by thorns recently forced
Onto his delicate head.
From here, I wince.
Only there can I comfort and be comforted.
I hear his lilting voices beckoning me
To come and be wrapped in his arms,
And soothed to eternal peace.

Elaine Carter

Dine With Me

Silently, we create
The figures which glisten
In the fallen blue.

Cold fingers
Press against her lips -
His childlike face
In solid matter - made her heart the

Hotter still.

Intrepid breath should
Suffocate,
Knowing how these tears will
Drown us.

But steel or silver
Pains
Consume us;
Blind, in molten pillows.

Kellyanne Chamberlain

Bar Lambs

They
Were watching me.
Looks fifty, she said,
Well, fifty five.

They
Were early thirties,
Spring lambs
And fair and full
And . . .
Well I can think fifty.

Smoothed hair forward.
Changed glasses to distance.

They
Were late thirties,
Shearlings
Plump, with dark roots,
But
I can still think fifty,
Say fifty-five.

Turned up hearing aid.

They
Were watching me.
Looks shifty, she said,
Like I said,
Shifty eyes.

Mutton

Alan Chesterfield

Crying With
A Smile On My Face

I bet you felt real smart
As you stood and packed your case
Packing all of your leather
Packing all of your lace
You said you needed time
You said you needed space
And you left me crying
With a smile upon my face

You found another guy
You found another place
Because he looks you in the eye
And makes your heartbeat race
You think I'm feeling sad?
Yes a real sad case
Because I'm crying with a smile
With a smile upon my face

Well, throughout your torrid game
I prepared to play my ace
I watched on Tenter Hooks
As your plan gathered pace
Because I found another girl
To take your place
That's why I'm
Crying with a Smile upon my face

Gary Cox

The Rebel

They were the state,
He was a free man.
They had the strength of opinion behind them,
But it's merely their opinion.
He has only his spirit.

They must be right, they are the state.
He must be silent.

He is only a voice.
Not severe, clear.
Not loud, proud.
Not wrong, strong.

And now there are no walls,
No walls, no doors.
Just blood on cold prison floors.

And?

And his spirit.

Gary Cox

PMT - Pre-Millennial Tension

There's chaos and confusion
Almost a revolution
Strikes, sit-ins, lock-outs
Too much to mention
And what could be the cause
Of the planet's sores?
PMT -
Pre-Millennial Tension!

It is said that the world
I coming to an end
Earthquakes, volcanoes, tidal-waves
Attract attention
But we say
'No, the world's not going to die'
It's just an attack of
PMT -
Pre-Millennial Tension!

The economists have broke us
The politicians try to choke us
And the ecclesiastics -
Well, they should get their pension!
For they are all being afflicted
By just one thing
PMT -
Pre-Millennial Tension!

It has been said that the soul
Has been replaced by cryogenics
On the whole
Plastic surgery, skin-grafts
Without pretension!
But from without
Let's look *within*
So that we begin

With
PMT -
Pre-Millennial Tension!

From all this we must depart
We could have lift-off
For a start
UFOs assisting our ascension
But from Earth's lot
We cannot stray
So let's give the game away
It's just
PMT -
Pre-Millennial Tension!

John Crowe

Eros Vs Thanatos

Hostile snow melting in the sun,
the frigid air warms.
In the fertile firm foundation
a lone flower bud forms.

The sun blazes in glory.
The flower blooms into a cascade of reds and pinks,
crimson, burgundy and cherry.
Blossoming and romancing.

But the breeze brings blustery bitterness
blowing the bleeding petals down.
One petal is left in loneliness.
Is there another seed sown?

The initial murderous snowflake drifts down from the
    skies,
the last petal withers away,
and the final light dies.

Darkness prevails. Triumphant.

Michelle Espley

Shed Another Skin

The wasp-stung, starved snakes lay
Ready for abuse.
With spiders crawling in their eyes,
With flies feeding on every pore.
They lay rotting on fields of cheap inhibitions
Starved by the devil they spawned.

I'll proceed with a dream of an envious scheme
To extract some equality from this intolerable wreck,
I'll pretend to be green with the chlorophyll of self-
    reliance,
And yet secretly be open to any half-hearted alliance
Which could raise me above this conscienceless place,
So that I am equal like the rest.

I'll shed another skin;
The bare bones exposed
Will illustrate the dryness
Of this vulnerable void,
I'll avoid sorrowful or whimsical charmers,
The snake charmer's pet fakes independence.
Let me devour this feeling of dependence.

Battered by your/our society;
The eternal sore thumb
Ripens with every generation.
That old plagiarised dream was never built in
Programmed incorrectly again and again.
Excreted from your sanity glands,
Your rank, rancid sweat;
Following behind, exposing half truths,
The green-skinned, charmed snake, bare bones youth.

Richard Evans

Retreating

Retreating into themselves
only sombre eyes speaking.
Holding hands, walking silently.

Reflecting on experience,
moments in the flow of their lives,
retreating into themselves.

They pause, remembering laughter,
walk faster, smiling inwardly,
holding hands, walking silently.

Will sorrow, forced separation,
prove more powerful than feelings,
retreating into themselves.

On low cliffs by the empty wards,
they look at the grey, rolling sea,
holding hands, walking silently.

An Institutionalised couple,
their security destroyed,
retreating into themselves,
holding hands, walking silently.

Robert E Fairclough

Paradise Island

Azure, turquoise seas
That sparkle in the golden sun
Pale, white sandy beaches
With tall tropical palm trees
Blowing in the light sea breeze.

Seagulls softly fly across the ripples of the ocean,
Splashes from dolphins disturbing the inky blue seas
Crafty crabs drift onto the pale sands
A paradise island is a heavenly summer's day.

Samantha Ferranti (11)

Assurances

Fear not the wolf:
Cruel hound whose incandescent eyes
Betray the evil in disguise,
But when you leave this world behind
He'll be your guide.

Fear not the bear:
Bellowing brute whose awesome force
Will render you a crumpled corpse,
But cut him open and you'll find
A man inside.

Fear not the serpent:
Slim seducer, hissing guile,
Who'll demonize you with a smile,
But one drop of his juices and
You shall be cured.

Then fear not me;
For, though I may have caused alarm
Initially, I mean no harm,
So now accept the human hand
That first seemed clawed.

Gillian Floyd

Through A Salty Window

Clouds hurry north,
Late for their rendezvous
With the wind-crazy plastic.
Gulls, wings finely tuned,
Move up-wind,
Improbably.

Quarry gapes, open for extraction.
Breakers scrub its man-shaped shore
Sucking a brown streak of residue -
Umbilical cord to breakwater,
Haven for ferries,
Mercifully.

On the seething, angry water
The ferry lifts, hovers, plunges,
Emerges proudly through bridge-high foam.
Creeps open-jawed to the terminal
To spew out brine-washed cars,
Triumphantly.

Sheltered from tides by a narrow beach track
The loch lies, calmer. Heathery grazing
Feeds hardy, bum-to-storm sheep.
On the flat green at the burn mouth
Birds wait, heads to wind,
Patiently.

In our gale-flattened garden
Sparrows seek shelter
Under brown-tipped clumps of bowing stems,
And a chubby hill-mouse, thief of bird food,
Darts home underground,
Impudently.

Wendy Gear

The Waiting Time

Through winter trees' fine fretwork
Glimpse the pale moon's imprint
Smudged on oyster sky;
White flash of wheeling gulls,
Banking in perfect choreography -
Then kaleidoscopic scatter
To alight on dark-ridged field;
Cupped in dip and hollow,
Water's silver gleam
Reflects soft February light,
Storm now abated.

A quiet time, this waiting time.

Ranks of snowdrops boldly challenge
Winter's iron heel; each snowy petal's edge
Heralding green spring.
Sheep creamy-white in pallid sun,
Their rounded forms echoed
In soft fleecy drifts of cloud,
Graze peacefully.

The earth waits . . .
Feeling the stirring, the vigour of new life:
Tight-folded buds; keen thrust of shoots
Beneath the soil.

Another waits
In quiet anticipation;
Smoothes white lacy shawl, still folded;
A new life waits . . .
Soon to know first glimpse of light,
First cradling of parents' love.
Soon . . .

Valerie Gough

Solitude Screaming

In this world where every remark is analysed.
your ideologies judged,
and the faintest trace of bigotry or intolerance
is condemned out of hand.
You are alone.

A world of transient, vicarious pleasure
and consumable art,
and all that at first seems vibrant and real
exists only as surface.
You are alone.

Where compassion and empathy invite scorn,
yet hostility is acceptable.
Where the very agencies that seek to socialise you
reinforce your alienation.
You are alone.

Where the definition of your sexuality
carries so much emphasis
within a society that is rotting from the inside,
infected with sexual deviance.
You are alone.

Within the rigid confines of this liberal culture,
forms of expression are easily censored.
Without the desire to escape the box to which I am
condemned,
my isolation is compete,
and I am alone . . .

. . . and I realise there is eloquence in screaming.

Nigel L Grain

Sweet Cushat

No eloquent words - can
Obliterate my anguish
And feelings - once private
Are now openly shared - for
In choosing your shelter
Your nescience
Made you unaware
That it too was mine.
And
Depriving you
Of your nesting time
Has borne me
With such melancholia
I seek forgiveness -
Knowing your name unites
With my conscience
Into eternity.

Irene Gunnion

Alone

The long wait by the
dumb phone
the silence of the unpressed
door bell
the indifferent postman who
ignores my letter box
adds to my sense
of isolation . . .
I feel unwanted
by the world
renounced
stripped
of my identity
I have become a thing in
the black hole
of non-existence
the dimension of nothingness.

Stephen Gyles

5th winner

The Depths Of Emotion

Crying is what men dream of,
When they are fast asleep,
When there is no one watching.
For reaction on the face,
There is just no way to tell,
Of emotion day to day,

In his heart, there seems no place,
For love or warm embrace,
But safety locks the key to dreams
And warm blood runs,
Beneath the seams.

Janine Harrington (14)

The Healing Process

I'm still searching for you,
flicking through my dreams every night
trying to capture your face.
I've almost forgotten,
it's fading at the edges,
the lines indistinct, the colours sepia brown.

Sometimes I see you in a shop doorway,
I call out, but when you turn
there's only a stranger with empty eyes.

I swore I'd never forget,
but time has a habit of shading in the detail to a blur.
My friends would say it's just as well,
all part of the healing process,

but they don't understand.
I want to hurt a little,
or I lose you forever.

Susan Hawkes

Vandalism

Your philosophy of life was simple.
Satisfied with four tins of dynamite
Plus a couple of packets of Swan;
The first top never cracked open, before
Midday, that was your daily routine and
It worked a treat.
You reached the height of four-score and two
Fantastic for a man who smoked like a chimney.
Then one Sunday afternoon the imps annoyed you;
Nobody heard the sound of smashing glass that
Shattered the panes of your greenhouse.
That's them with the black woolly hats,
You explained to a concerned neighbour.
They've no respect for other people's property.
Now my plants are floating like dead ducks on a pond.
The parents are to blame,
Said the pugnacious-type neighbour.
Then with brassiness said,
Leave this one to me old chap.
He stormed towards the imps and returned clutching
What looked like three birds' nests in three . . .
Black woolly hats.

Francis Hughes

D For Disaster

She drove into darkness
A wreck
But the cry of the wolf
Could only be heard
By hills with ears
While the deaf river
Babbled its own kind of language
As the moon hung like a light bulb
Over sleeping Edinburgh.
Asleep in her water-bed
Allowing the river to trickle
Sweet language
Of her own art
In water colours.
She was tongue tied
To tell the hanging moon
She had already sketched her paradise
In a heaven round the twinkling stars.
After the flicker of light
There was no more.

Francis Hughes

Holding The Hand Of Fear

There is no comfort here,
My soul can but shiver
Holding the hand of fear.

I drop a single tear
In the flowing river,
There is no comfort here.

The mountainside is sheer,
I can only quiver
Holding the hand of fear.

Love's hunger is too clear
For without a giver
There is no comfort here.

There is no one to steer
The nightmares that dither
Holding the hand of fear.

Into despair I peer
And into a void slither,
There is no comfort here
Holding the hand of fear.

Pat Isiorho

Graveside

Stillness.
The hushed roar of traffic.
Breath of fresh air
Beneath the trees.

Quietness.
Whispered phrases -
Prayers and the weather.

Creativity.
Flowers arranged perfectly.
Artistry uncovered -
Talent discovered.

Sadness.
Snippets of lives recalled
Jumbled memories
Framed in our minds.
Frozen in time.

Laura Joyce (16)

Wing

You've been hit!
A rush of feathers courts the road
wing thrashing trying to lift your shattered body.
You raise your head
side on from the numbing asphalt
taking fleeting glances at the passing of life
then still descends.
The stiffening wind captures a wing
and leaves it raised like an epitaph, a swan song
till the first bus arrives.
An old lady feeds a jostling crowd
of fellow pigeons on the square close by . . .
atoned by showering seed.
Tugging children point out your warm remains
to their mothers as they walk past the place where
a wing once thrashed.

John Kearney

Megalomaniac's Elevenses

I play your patronising games . . .
Yes, you make me feel useless
Yes, you make me feel small.
Insignificant, inferior, incapable,
Stupid.
I've never liked myself much
Sensitive as hell
You reduce me to tears
Yet . . .
You chew on my confidence with relish
A biscuit ground to crumbs
Under the heel of your sharp tongue
But fight I can,
And fight I will,
Because if I let you crawl under my skin
You'll linger like eczema,
And start to spread . . .

Sarah Kent

In The Course Of Time

Anticipation concentrates the mind

Two steps ahead of me, dreams of people not yet
    born in cities
not yet built, on hot, lazy days not yet gone by, they stare
back at me, shadowing my life in the here and now.

There's nothing quite like waking up to what you
    knew was going
to be there, to the same old yesterday surroundings.
Nothing quite so despairing as that.
The same old vase on the mantelpiece, same old
    colour of curtains
hiding only the same old view, making the morning
    seem more
like a brash extension of the night before than the 'fresh
beginning, whole new day' sensations we have been
    conditioned to believe in.

It's time to move on then.
Time now to change the view, buy a new vase, swap
    the curtains for a blind.
Until, in the course of time, the same old depression
    sets in,
turning the new to old, painting grey all what was white,
installing hate where love once blossomed.

Repeat the process until you stop breathing.

Gary Knapton

Five Thieves

Stand, blind friend and sunward face.
How may I puncture your eyes
That you may see again?
Who has snatched your certainty?

Now your cotton wool tongue
Absorbs without recognition.
Thirst and drink with swift dissatisfaction
This tasteless life.

You shattered and solitary splinter,
Your fumbling hands are numb.
Your joy is lost to time and momentary
Like mercury through your senseless fingers.

You listen but the world screams mutely
At a sealed consciousness hearing only emptiness
Within a vast silence
Instead of an answered prayer.

I shall smash a steely bolt to crack your nostril wide
That you may sniff the truth is all
Around itself inside.
The truth is not outside itself inside.

Jose Lacey

5th
winner

Titanic

Cocooned in orange plush, obscenely safe,
In false cinematic twilight;
Light leaping out of nowhere,
Dizzying the frozen yet titillated onlooker.
The popcorn-crunching crowd have eaten myth.

Beached siren
Your seaweed ropes,
Drowned umbilicals,
Attach you to the seabed's vast placenta.
Your rusticles drape you like a sleeping shroud.

The knife-edge of your bow; the knife plunged into mud.
A spherical light fixture sprouts a sea pen;
Many-fingered: a poignant Medusa.
A high-button shoe rests close by.
White ocean crockery, ghost porcelain -

Appurtenances of a sunken pelagian people.
Your silt bed, more than two miles below,
Private even now,
Refuses to yield its virgin treasure still.
A valedictory message, torn from a pocket calendar,

Forced into a cold clasping hand -
A desperate flutter of paper.
Strobe, like a marine rapist, raking the ocean floor;
Invasion of the depths below.
Your one-way virgin voyage, inescapable.

The night was a still pool of indigo.
The berg glided silently by,
Lethal as a shark's fin, with terrible finality.
The pin-prick stars, flowers of light,
Averted their eyes respectfully.

Charlotte Leather

A Disaster

A shirt that was once white now brown and half-undone,
　　tie loosened and hair scruffy.
His shoes kicked off at the entrance as he makes his
　　way to his territory.
His smelly feet are mounted on the table, TV remote
　　at hand.

The loud sounds of commentators and spectators
　　followed by a joyous scream of *goal!*
　　Invade my thoughts.
All peace and quiet is snatched away from the home,
　　selfish in my opinion.

Travelling only to drain the kitchen of all its supplies.
Countless numbers of goals fill the evening's atmosphere.
Now he's fast asleep on the couch, saliva sipping
　　from the corner of his mouth.

Feet still up, hands clutching a large bag of crisps,
　　Coke spilt all over the table, socks and shoes in
　　the same position as they were before and
　　TV still on.

A disaster in its own right.

Natacha Leopold (14)

Ugly

I came home yesterday to find
that you were ugly,
your warm, welcoming smile had descended
to a gap-tooth winter graveyard,
heavened by hollow moons of black.

Only that morning I had kissed
the most perfect woman the world would allow,
all roses and radiance,
all soft focus and smiles,
all mine and all important.

Now I wake this morning to find
that you are ugly,
your firm, naked body having been replaced
by a foul, bloated carcass
bathed in impure white.

Your voice no longer stirs me
or rivets with every word,
your touch, still filled with shivers,
beckons a rage or the fear
or perhaps even both.

I wish I could go back to the breakfast table,
the day before today, and look across
at your deceitful eyes, finding you
had nothing to hide and nothing
to hurt me with.

But now I open the bathroom door,
freshly shaven and smelling of Brut,
to find you standing, weeping,
hair like a million fitting centipedes,
face like a bag of smashed crabs,

ugly;
but he probably doesn't think so.

Christopher Long

London's Homeless

They wander through the
Dark, unpleasant, starry night;
Seeking for solitude and
Somewhere to stay.

They haunt a cardboard box,
Steal a mattress and
Ramble through a pile of
Waste.

They try to speak, cannot
Be heard.
They try to smile, cannot
Be seen.

Surrounded by the inhumanity
And wealth of people,
They remain unknown.

Often they are seen lying
On the floor
Cold, tired and weak.
Deprived of life's comforts.

They seem anguished and
Betrayed
Striving for independence
Praying for understanding.

They stand in tears
Grieving among the impoverished
Faces of society.

Some begin to move
Others freeze motionless.
They have nowhere to go
Nowhere to hide.

Abandoned, secluded, afraid
They battle on.

Georghios Makasis

Image

Do not intrude here
I want to be left
To throw my stones
In the water
I am casting shadows
Not spells
Not nets
I watch them break
Through the surface
And disappear
Without form
Without breath
Without name
My fingers cannot
Catch cannot
Hold and feel the
Warmth sink between
Skin and vein
I do not want to
Remember my image
I do not want to
Retrieve the identity
I see it retract
And split like an atom
Into the endless matter
That does not matter much to me.

Sharon Marshall

One Slave Too Many

The locked door
And that tight space,
Your eyes reading me,
Enjoying my shame, though you're motionless now
And not touching me now.
But your mouth and tongue were all mine when I died.
Bound and pierced.
Your drink-puffed lips
Will extinguish the flame in me,
My light will go out,
Blackness will become my only dream
And I
Won't even have been born.

Tonight
A sandstorm in a desert, my throat,
As I pace the floor, reach for my coat.
The floorboard creaks,
My mind freaks . . .
No help now, I've got to get
Out!

Forlorn as the November cold,
Battered as a wet-worn autumn leaf,
Wind-torn and dying.
On the step that I can't leave
Drawn to the centre of the slab
A blood victim,
Waiting for you, my only certainty,
To open the door and let the light out,
And blow my life away.
One word will do it.

There will not be another night, no other sight.
I will never be born.

Linda Martin

Poets

We are impractical
Vacuous, lost
In this practical world,
Wild, tempest-tossed.

But our words peal
Through the centuries long;
Loud words, and bold words,
Sweet words of pity
For the herd and Canaille

Whom we raised from the dust
And the polluted sty.

Strong words and bold words;
Words trumpet-tongued
That peal through the ages
Inspiring the sages;
Moving the rabble
To hurl down the tyrant
And make themselves lord.

Oh! These are the dreamers
So peaceful, so mild.
Who let loose the torrent
Of words, dangerous, wild!

John J McAlister

The Estate Children

On the wall
a steady green arch
open as a Great White's jaws
hoping to swallow
the children of the council estate

Heavy bins on wheels
in twos
a giant's binoculars
almost invisible metallic grey
lightly dusted with car fumes

A broken bike
minus the handlebar
leans lazily against railings
the rust of the spokes
and frame
betray the fact it's not autumn

An ashen tree
bending to an archer's strain
black at the roots
has been set alight
and been allowed to burn out

On this bench
scratched names
do not hinder comfort
but face this way
drawn to a distant shriek
hemmed in by damp bricks.

Andy McPheat

It Only Takes One Seed . . .

The field was simply there.
I passed it, watching seasons:
soft brown to lush green,
into glittering gold, and neat rolls.
A constant, rural, timeless scene;
a pleasing field I mused upon,
travelling from here to there.

Today complacency is rocked,
this traveller's bubble has been burst!

Monsters have descended overnight,
grubbing, grabbing the soft brown soil,
regurgitating it from ghastly mouths
to lorries, travelling concrete paths
the sooner to destroy the scene,
they journey sightless through the dust.

If only I had known last summer's end
your scented fronds were waving, waving goodbye . . .

Now you're scarred: great gaping veins
of gravel criss-crossing in stony banks.
No live-saving bypass here,
only crushing pain of threatened death,
as your heart is pounded and mauled.
The beat of nature's rondo is no more.

But wait - my field has depths unknown:
the monsters halt, wide mouthed;
metallic dinosaurs captured in time.
As for me, I too must stop,
enthralled, I stare,
halting my journey from here to there.

I gaze upon an awesome scene.
The field is bleeding, throbbing, ruby red.

Down the arteries of grit and sand
pours wonderful, miraculous life!
Poppies dancing; poppies preening;
poppies laughing, scorning, gleaming;
poppies in their tens of thousands,
glowing, sowing, proudly flowing
mocking man's attempt at maiming,
pulsating heralds, burning, flaming!

Clever field, you knew the time
to bring your treasure out from hiding!
Kept it buried down the years,
then let it burst upon the land,
to prove that nature's hold is greater,
purer, finer than mercenary man's;
exemplifying in this deed,
nothing surpasses the strength
of one seed.

Elizabeth S McWilliam

I Know Not Who I Am

My identity is lost,
I know not who I am,
You tell me I am black,
My mother is,
Black,
Yet I am not.
You tell me I am white,
My father is,
White,
Yet I am not.
Mother, I am different from you,
You can only teach me to be black.
Rich Westerner,
I am lost in your country,
Father, I am different from you,
You can only teach me to be white.
Unfortunate child,
I am lost in your country.

Dawna-Mechellé Lewis

Alone

I am alone.
Only my dreams do haunt me,
Silence echoes in my ears,
A gentle breeze brushes past me,
I am alone,
Only my dreams do haunt me,
I raise my stormy eyes to the looming grey sky,
I watch the black clouds swirling angrily overhead,
I am alone,
Only my dreams do haunt me,
Rain starts to fall gently, quickly gaining speed,
Its beat matching the rhythm of my heart,
I am alone,
Only my dreams do haunt me,
The flowers seem to close up, shrink into themselves,
I cannot shrink into myself,
I am alone,
Only my dreams do haunt me,
I am vulnerable in this open field,
The flowers seem to have disappeared,
All bright colour washed away,
I am alone,
Only my dreams do haunt me,
My tears seem to go unnoticed as the rain falls,
My own salty tears mix with the earth's tears until
they are one,
But I am still alone in this field,
And have only my dreams to haunt me.

Rowshownara Miah (16)

Perfect Herd

An electric impulse opens
the door.
A thought, a concept
to inspire the masses;
'Create salvation in the pain of life.'
An electric impulse embraces
the notion,
Carries the message
from mouth, to ear, to brain;
Transmitter. Radar. Terminal.
An electric impulse then lays
the first brick
of the new found lord.
press the keys of the computer race
to watch the masses flock and
worship at the feet of their newly created
eternal deity.

Matthew Moon

Night Walker

Bricks are hard
Like words at the side of the house
Climbing where chimneys
Mine and next door display
The littered tablecloth
From which we like to measure near and far
Or watch the floral moon take out a star
Whatever. This arrangement going on
Unmindful of our quarrel.

The chimneys are friends
Companions in mutual agreement
And twin walls from below
Seem to lean together
Narrowing the gap, the gap, the gap.
Their kitchen window spills some light
Sticks of orange march the garden trees
Into a wayward sorting for the night.

Unwanted voices
Do they suspect I am out here
Watching our friendly chimneys?

Rosemary Muncie

A Promised Land

Sad streets now stand where once before
fields of barley held their sway.
New towns erupt and cast their ash
on plots of unresisting clay.
The winding country lanes of old
no longer meet the needs
of traffic built to travel
at suicidal speeds.
Man's axe has razed the leafy spires
and caused the earth to die
Now forests of another kind
reach up to scrape the sky;
spewing smoke and silent death
which, carried by the wind
returns to shroud the sleeping soil
and all that lies within.
Must man destroy what God creates
can time forgive this shame,
will those who follow keep their faith
and make the world a better place
where man can live with God again?

John Notley

Suburban Lives

A quiet couple, keeping to themselves,
Behind high fences working on a dream:
A garden with water, shrubs and trees. She,
Far more outgoing, more relaxed it seems -
Shopping with neighbours, chatting of her schemes.
He was so reserved - people were off-put -
A nod or wave as he drove off was all
We got. One morning he appeared barefoot,
Dishevelled and a wheelie bin in tow,
Looking for the refuse truck. Embarrassed,
Caught unawares, he blurted out, 'I don't
See any bins put out.' Wild eyed, harassed,
he asked, 'Am I too late?' 'Early,' I said
Adding as he relaxed, 'By just a day!'
We laughed, finding a bond, a small thing shared -
A friendship almost started in that way.

But now he's dead. I found out just by chance -
Almost too late to send 'Sincere regrets.'
Died at the weekend: a bloody smash, she
Had seen it all - something she won't forget.
Will she go on, trying to catch a dream?
(A pond half dug and walls to raise between)
Or will she feel her life here's at an end:
All hope lost in a manner unforeseen?

The house is silent now while she's away
Staying with friends - the nightmare on replay.
The garden waits, two roses by the door:
Emblems of what was, if she returns once more.

Patrick B Osada

The Visit

Frail fingers
fret and twitch the rug marked
-*Ward 9 Men* -
Nurse folds about your chair.

Grieving
I watch the mindless movement
of those hands,
age stained now
yet strangely soft and childlike:
the hands
that plucked my innocence
made me wise.

I reach out
and clasp your fingers:
you gaze
at me
through me
past me.

Nurse tells me
you are happy in your world:
it is only I
who rage
at the nothingness in your soul.

I urge you to feel
pain, anger, passion:
instead
you smile -
benign
serene
so bloody indifferent.

Kit Pawson

Consequences

I have my poem,
Wretched thing
In perfect order;
Rehearsed
Reckless precision
Of the sure.
Fashioned
For a purpose
It lies
On the threshold
Of my tongue
I have forged
My weapon
Loaded
With meaning,
Meaning to hurt.
And I will
Use it
Though I know
The pain
Corrosion and regret
Since I have used
Similar weapons
Before.
A game;
Predicted Consequences
That fools like me
Who have not learned
To be loved
Have to unfold
And read
To the end.

John Powls

Spring Into Light

Wreathed in the aroma
of new sandal leather.
Fluvial freedom from a feather
on each curious foot.
Liberated with gazelle like grace,
into nature and space.
Away from the yokes and chains
of restriction,
negation of friction,
rules and sterility.
From hearth and home
to the warmth of the barn.
To hedges and ditches,
mosses and lichens,
soulmates who beckoned,
as earth opened her arms
to welcome the dawn,
salute to rebirth,
with a ripening yawn.

Stephanie Rankin

Seascape

Exploring his canvas of unrelieved white,
he guided the brush in his hand
to paint iridescence in ultramarine
with flecks if sea danced over land.
His eyes understood this incredible scene
of pebbles on glittering sand.

The shadowy background was sombre and dull
but glimmering rays from the sun
shot beams on the crest of a hovering wave
and half-light beneath every one.
A luminous sheen on the billowing deep
enlivened the work he had done.

The artist was reaching the edge of his world
discovering boats on the sea
with shifting reflections in palest of tones
and sails tempestuous and free.
Each stroke of his brush was made with such care
it looked in proportion to me.

Forgetting the patchwork of streaks on himself,
he skilfully laboured all day.
A towering headland soared up to the clouds
in ochre and umber or grey.
Completing a yacht in vermilion and rust
He folded his easel away.

The seascape was mounted and hung on a wall.
When days became longer and cold
he lifted his eyes from the smouldering fire
to travel triumphant and bold
up towering cliffs to the crest of his world.
This picture will never be sold.

Nancy Reeves

Woman In Love

When she fell in love
It was for all time,
And the Gods
In their silent understanding,
Allowed the planets
To spin out of control,
Beyond the ones of rhyme;
And they cried
In their constant watching,
As he betrayed her
Leaving her to see,
Only the last smile that ran
Through running rain
And misty windows of the dawn,
Long before the day began;
And oh! how she would feel
In morning the pull of apricot moons,
To tiptoe past
The remnants of burnt sienna stars
Before the night should fall,
Around the gowns of dewy Saturn;
And sometimes the burning leaves
Of Autumn
Would come in early May,
Leaving only
Windswept memories of summer sands
Far out of her reach and play;
For in the Garden of her heart
Still grew the tree of bittersweet,
Where she would sing a sad song
Of gentle scented reminding,
In the hopes that he would
Come back home once more to stay,
And the harvest sun
Would hide for shame its blushing face,

For it had no song upon the meadow
Only the moments that burned the flame;
And in August upon a ghost lake
She would haunt like a white swan,
As evening breezes
Held their whispered strain,
For a Princess was in the passing
Long before the winter ever came.

Norman Royal

The Demolition Man

Most of the time
she knows he loves her
in his own fashion.
Quietly.
Except every once in a while
when he does a demolition job
on her emotions.
Crumbling them neatly to dust
like any old chimney stack.

Most of the time
his good points shine over
their marriage like a light.
A beacon.
Except every now and then
when he does a demolition job
on her happiness.
Eroding it slowly and surely
as any sea-lashed coastline.

Most of the time
she's happy with her
lot in life.
Even content.
Except every once in a while
when he does a demolition job
on her dreams.
With his own brand of mental cruelty
delivered with a smile.

Maureen Reynolds

The Cry Of The Forest Fairy

(Song for Danielle)

'Life,' she said
To open sky and absent friends,
'Was once danced across the face
Of earth's sweet garden,
Upon the wings of fancy
And tiptoe finding ends of daisy.
Where once,
I lived and loved
Under elfin moons of burnt sienna,
And played aplenty
Until pixie surprises of morning's song
Caught the shady leaves
Of emerald ever;
And I held cover for
All the lonely hearts,
That wandered on through the hazy days
To find me,
And I cried when they did too
In falls of dewy bower;
And I died a thousand deaths
For every tree cut down needlessly,
Leaving my tears
Still in the hearts of golden daffodils
To grow anew,
In fields of reminding lemon
And groves of bluebell's blue.
And in my last breath
I will let fall
The scent of willow's core,
To cover over the eyes of ash and hazel
Before the sacred oak of now lies bleeding,
And I am no more.'

Norman Royal

The Abortion Of A Catholic Priest

Tonight
I watched the television
with mum,
protected, in front of the warm dark fire
slowly dying in the night.
Conflict
on the news. Anger.
Condemn/nation.
Ripped from society a Catholic priest
stood with his father.
Money.
Support. A single innocent life saved.
But society declared
'The bribe and persuasion was inappropriate.'
Oppressive. Baby Benedict
Johnson
clawed at the screen and laughed
with his mum.
Protected by a loosely wrapped blanket
and another option.

Natalie Russell

Patio Lizard

There is a sunny patio in Greece,
With bleached burned stones before an orange wall,
Bright flowers that bloom in terra cotta pots,
Where large brown lizards sit to view it all.

A Grecian love god in white shorts all frayed,
Comes out to oil his beautiful physique,
While lager louts from Britain are dismayed,
To see a bloke so edible and Greek.

The lizard stares at them with topaz eyes,
Thinking how ugly are the whole species,
With hair upon their chests and heads and thighs,
I am superior he thinks to these.

But then they are God's creatures too like me,
Beauty we know may only be skin deep,
Even so I'm very pleased to be,
A smooth skinned reptile, topaz eyed and Greek.

Kathleen Scatchard

The Cave

Comforting for life's raw pain, grief,
this cave, this silent peaceful place,
far off the beaten track by bush,
near the shore of an island lake,
the entrance camouflaged by ferns,
a fawn shade of volcanic rock,
between boulders a winding path,
sunrays filtering through fern fronds,
light focusing on a deep jade pool,
pure cool water, refreshing, sweet;
Time in this cave for reflecting, praise
God's presence, beauty, calming joy.

Virginia Schlegel

Venice At Night

Listen
as water kisses
the belly of boats
of this drowning
moon-wrapped maze
where shadows slip
from out of view
to disappear
forever.

The tired feet
of travellers lost
are caught by
echoed walls and
dark sweet smells
slide from a door
seducing them to enter.
Inside are rows of
cut-glass bulbs
steamed sides of
hot-spiced ruby.

Outside the air
is weaving frost;
its legacy of loveliness
before the dawn
with blood-warm hands
wrings out the
white-thread shawl.

Eleanor Scott Plummer

Passionate Destruction

Romeo and *Juliet*,
How does the world perceive your love?
How do I see you,
Anthony and *Cleopatra?*
Metallic revolvers at one hundred paces
Strike bullets into the fire
Where death becomes the *'Cu'* of *'pid'*
And cats of purity lap in security
Staring into the gun of a barrel
Silver power in the wake of a bloody carol
Where love and pain fights fist to fist
And daggers spear the crystal execution
Serenaded by the choir of satanic angels
Of no worldly relation
Pins elevated to the status of bloody weapons
In a domain of obsessive pain
Dolls reform to soldiers in a drama of voodoo
Painted faces ameliorate in the era of war paint
Harmony defends itself in the name of discord
Metallic revolvers at one thousand miles
Guns and missiles
The torrid toys of selfish desires
Starves love of its infinite carnal fires.

Louisa Shilton

A Lesson In Love

He looked at me,
I looked at him,
He winked my way,
So I gave him a grin.
I batted my eyelashes,
He flicked his hair,
For flirting,
He had a natural flair.
As he walked past,
He brushed at my side,
I imagined myself,
As his blushing bride.
I thought of a date,
With the man of my dreams,
But he had other ideas,
Or so it seemed.
He passed me a note,
'Not to offend'
But he wanted the phone number,
Of my very best friend.

Chloe Shoniwa

Teddy's Eye

Teddy's only got one eye,
he uses it to see,
what happens in the dead of night,
the things they do to me,
I'm not allowed to make a sound,
or it will spoil their game,
and silence tells me not to cry,
as innocence is slain.

The pain is sometimes very bad,
but I never, ever weep,
as cold hearts leave me lying,
beneath the cold, cold sheets,
their game is called our secret,
and I mustn't ever say,
not even in my prayers at night,
to give the game away.

I know that this must end one day,
and I know I'm not alone,
for somewhere up in heaven,
Christ sits upon His throne,
and weeps for all the children,
who suffer in this way,
and one day he will rescue me,
and one day I'll be free.

Mike Smith

Potato Pickers

There is a grey inner anger of darkness
Rumbling under surface tension,
A sword-shark streak of steel
Slashes the black-blanketed tempest
Shedding silver shards of broken glass.

The rain beats across the landscape
Falling in sheets of sodden splinters
Mud splatters in puddles of sow-slop
Blinding the eye to the rich soil sinking
Below the heavy weight of wellington boots.

The ice-numb fingers grub among the earth
Scouring the sludge for a few rich potatoes.
The water runs in rivulets down the verges.
A labourer blasphemes the maker of bad weather
The atmosphere explodes with a roar of vengeance.

A disgruntled clapped-out tractor belches black smoke
Against a filthy sky of rinsed-out dirty linen.
The wooden pallets and plastic buckets are a burden
Of splashing water spilling out onto saturation
Is there nowhere that is not water?

The backs of the potato-pickers arch against the incline
Straddling the sludge of a washed-out trench
Slipping on the slope in a slurry of mud.
A day's labour for a meagre pittance, a loaf of bread and
A bottle of wine are the wages for a rotten crop.

Two holiday-makers stop the car to find directions
Scour at a crumpled map then stare at the huddle
Of figures stooping over the rain-soaked earth.
They feel apologetic for the Jersey Royals eaten at lunch
Then drive on against the rain in search of a new location.

R J Stallon

Dried Up And Out Of Mind

Bumping along the Roo road from Sindo
spastically jiggled by rut and by stone
we make lots of dust but little more than walking pace
and I am battered into feeling the need for stronger
    shock absorbers.

On either side of this dirt track road the maize stands
as yellow paper sculpture useless long before harvest
though the millet still struggles on to some grim maturity.
This will be a lean year here. Again, it seems.
In every rough cut field and patch of shrub traditional
houses squat: their mud-dung walls and grass
    thatched roofs
healthier than an infested shanty-slum by Nairobi
but with no rain for man nor maize there is scarcely
    sustenance.
Yet, tourist brochure beautiful, Lake Victoria lies not a
    mile away
a sea on the far side of the moon in poverty:
this is too far away for anyone to care.

Dead ahead a skeletal young man dressed only in
    dirt and rolling eyes
totters towards us, arms outstretched like a toddler.
A local tragedy, I hear: he will try to latch on to our
    pick-up truck.
His cheek is surely within caressing distance
just as I swerve brutally out of his reach
glance into his wild unknowing eyes
glimpse all that is irrational beyond control
am wrenched by stark injustices
shudder somewhere deep inside snap shut my
    sensitivities

and, in crashing of pothole, gears, bones and conscience,
lurch on.
With and without relief
I watch him blend into our frantic dust,
the scene dissolving fast in my shaking rear-view mirror.

Stephen Eric Smyth

Charity Jump

Queen of the sky, her eyes ignite at the space
Of space that tears her breath
As she leaps to float
New-born and cradles down to earth
Over Ffos Y Ffin and the muffled sea.
Facing the land that made her,
Spread-eagled, splints along her thighs, she rides
Above the kites that lurch from the Saturday hill.
Still mute with joy she sees her house, 'Pant Cefn',
Her lover, child. Two arms embrace
The drift of sheep on shapely green
Before Brigantia's breath, a sudden roar
Sweeps her north and listing
On the mercy of emptiness.

This is not the plan.
A martyr's tear drags from her eyes, her burden locked
Unbillowing. Falling past the ancient trees,
Log cabins with retirement teas and news east of the hills.
A place of strangers, sheltered host
Of cries lost to the foreign breeze.
The layered humus, after centuries
Shivers to the breech death. Welcome.
To the silence of a myriad small things.

The couple from Todmorden make their way
On unworked ankles. Too much armchair cosy,
Their fingers knotted mistletoe, clinging
To a life endured but now forgotten
As the forest fills their shoes.
'Happen it were a bird,' he says, his tired eyes
Already in the Otherworld.
His stick divining in the Sidh for gold,
While above, the palaver of rooks is stilled,
For the Greater Queen's whispering note.
And they sing as though this was the only voice.
Their lullaby.

Sally Spedding

Are Such Men Still Out There?

Berliners sunbathing by city lakes
Women huddled trembling in a wood
Half-naked men bludgeoned to death by crowbar
Burying all human concerns beneath a larger goal

The smart floral dresses smile broadly
As the killers stand for their anthem
Unswerving dedication
Hand-crafted methods of liquidation

Not an inexplicable eruption of evil
But the marriage
Of bureaucratic determination and routine malice
Always ready for recruitment

Singular horrors
I know not
Singular people to commit them
I think not

How much did those sunbathers know?
Disappearance of common conscience beware
Such men
Are still out there.

B A Stone

Departures

A sudden surge of anger which I blamed on hormones
    and the house erupted
Like a volcano; blood rushed to my head it seemed gushing.
My tongue was as sharp as a razor
It really must have stung you, my darling, like a
    demented wasp
But pride prevailed whilst worried words followed me
    out of the door embedded in my early morning mind;
the sleepless night of tossing and turning, hearing the
    dawn chorus
the hammering rain beating on the bedroom windows
 whilst you slept soundly, oblivious to my pain . . .

I was a whirlwind when I awoke.

Now: walking briskly, I checked with God: 'Was it my fault?'
Swiftly, the answer came loud, lucid: 'Yes!'
And I could *still* stop in my tracks, retrace my hurried
    steps to find you pacing the floor like a caged Big Cat.
Or I could run to the nearest phone kiosk . . .
but I had a bus to catch,
inside my heart was racing as I paced the lakeside
    looking for the
 summer instead of incessant June rain and drains gurgling;
the gushing rush hour of Milton Keynes as traffic hissed
    past splattering miserable moaning pedestrians.
The lake loomed merely as a blur as tears welled up
    within my eyes
the heron stood stretching but unnoticed as my pace
    on the pathway quickened.

A sharp pang! I remembered nothing more.
Life's tortuous trail terminated.
You would never know because I was too busy to say,
'Sorry.'

Judy Studd

That Sense Of Failure

I called it
Life's a bitch
That first book of mine.
I sent it abroad, full of hope.
It came back.

And it was blackness - inside.
Where was the one
Who, up to then,
Had thought she was strong . . .
Where was she? I felt sad.

So sad inside. And so alone . . .
An awful kind
Of aloneness . . .
Never before experienced.
Crushed, I was - inside.

Lost. I had opened my heart
For the good of no-one.
For the good of me, I now say . . .
Life's a bitch was written for me.
Those years, those moments,

Have taught me so much.
And the one who, up to then,
Had thought she was strong . . .
Now, truly, is
Strong. I know me. I know me well.

My thoughts, my words,
Help me along the way.
Life's a bitch. Actually,
It's not that simple, I now say . . .
Life's a friend too.

Claire-Lyse Sylvester

Time

Where has it gone
I hear people say
Can it be true
That time's slipped away
Time that has gone
Like the wind in the trees
The spinning and dancing
Of leaves as they weave . . .
And fall to the soft brown earth . . .

Where has it gone
I hear people say
Each second, each moment
Melts into day
Love . . . joy . . . and pain
Each moment gone
Relentlessly . . . cruel . . . moving on
Until the world stops turning . . .

Gwen Tominey

Ninth Symphony

A thousand milk teeth
suck against the peel,
while you throw stone speeches at me.
And I stand alone in the garden
throwing stones at the glass.
Hoping to shatter
the silence of ice between us.

You turn and a black cloud follows,
while I fix a new zipper
to my bleeding lips, afraid to speak.

You cry frozen tears,
each one painful after the other,
and I walk around wearing a blindfold.
Blind and deaf to your sometime needs.
I have hung my uniform in the window
for all to see, and my chest of love
has been replaced with old clothes.

We now speak a foreign language
neither of us understands.
As we tread on each other's toes in this box we share.

Sophie Tomlinson

Slack Alice

She kicks off her shoes as she lights up a fag,
making some tea while taking a drag.
She watches telly as she eats her curry,
the bills pile up but she's not worried.
She drinks too much and doesn't sleep,
she parties hard and never eats.
Boys or girls, she doesn't care,
Slack Alice does it everywhere.
Slack Alice sits on the stairs,
taking calls from men that swear.

Her daddy left when she was four,
her mum's OK but she's a whore.
She never cries when she goes home,
Slack Alice waits till she's alone.
Slack Alice crawls into bed,
a Tuesday night and she's off her head.
She turns over and she's not alone,
some young lad who should be at home.
She feels so rough,
she's four months' gone,
she can't remember where she went wrong.
She's all dressed up and on the game,
some men drive by and shout her name.
She turns around and heads for home,
half way she meets a bloke she knows.
Fifteen quid for half an hour,
he shoots up, she takes a shower.

She lost the baby and she moved away,
she didn't mind she had bills to pay.
She's giving up and she's getting tired,
the things she's lost, the cheats and liars.
Last week Slack Alice lay in bed,
bodies heaving, but her passion was dead.

She had a few drinks and got out of her head,
she made a decision and wrote down what she said.
'My name is Alice, I am 24.
I don't know my dad and my mum is a whore.
I'm sick of this life and the things I have done.
I'm fighting a battle that cannot be won'.

My friend Slack Alice jumped off a cliff,
cursing God and the life she had lived.
There is a Slack Alice inside all of us,
we try and forget the things that she does.
We must not ignore her or she will persist,
and our problems will become the only reasons we
    exist…

Becky Uttley

In The Street

in the street - a momentary vision
on the periphery of ability
smile and laughter
tight lycra on shiny limb

in the street - a momentary vision
no longer aware of myself
our eyes met - then passed
cascading through time

in the street - a momentary vision
could feel her energy
my impulse - my desire
a longing to hold and be aroused

in the street - a momentary vision
clear cut expressions given to no-one
low involuntary breathing
then extreme primal instinct

in the street - a momentary vision
picturing life together
courting - marrying - divorcing - dying
and then she was gone
and gone forever

Barry Weldon

Two Years On

Security fades. I am not happy.
Castigated. Maligned. Alone.
Memories conspire to hold me.
Unwanted images free to roam.
Dancing before my sleepy eyes,
former friends and evil lies.
In court I would be acquitted.
In life I am outwitted.

Pleas of innocence sound so false.
She listens to them, she can't hear me,
ignoring words redolent and coarse,
telling her what I am and aim to be.
Our glorious future planned platonically
has gone, is dead, but not for me.
Punishment by absence seems unjust, unfair.
Please don't make me care.

P Williams

Psychiatrist

She says,
'Tell me when you feel most relaxed,'
'What do you mean?' he asks,
'Can you recall an activity,
Or place you fell most . . .'
Interrupting he says,
'I see, I am sorry I was not concentrating.'
'Take your time' she says.
'When I am walking in the woods, alone.'
'Close your eyes
Imagine you are walking in the woods,
What can you see?
Do you feel the wind?
Can you hear the leaves rustling?'
He takes over, 'Yes, yes I can.'
He composes himself,
'It is autumn, the trees are magnificent
A melting pot of colour,
As the wind blows, some spiral towards earth.'
'What else?'
'I can see the leaves forming a blanket
Of golden brown and fire red,
As I spin around
All I can hear is my own feet crunching the leaves.'
There is a long silence,
'What are you thinking now?'
'The forest is dying
And all I can do is marvel at its beauty.'
'Does that make you feel sad?'
He slightly frowns while searching for understanding,
Then quickly relaxes breaking into a slight smile.
'No, not, at all, in the spring
The forest will be reborn again.
No, I do not feel sad, just hopeful for the future.'

Paul Willis

INFORMATION

We hope you have enjoyed reading this book - and that you will continue to enjoy it in the coming years.

If you would like to enter this year's competition, drop us a line or give us a call and we'll be happy to send you a free information pack.

Contact:

Forward Press Top 100 Information
Remus House
Coltsfoot Drive
Woodston
Peterborough
PE2 9JX

Tel: 01733 898102
Fax: 01733 313524